LEGACY *of a* LEGEND

Spiritual Treasure from the Heart of Edward Payson

EDWARD PAYSON

SOLID GROUND CHRISTIAN BOOKS

SOLID GROUND CHRISTIAN BOOKS
PO Box 660132, Vestavia Hills, AL 35266
(205) 978-9469
solid-ground-books@juno.com
http://solid-ground-books.com

Legacy of a Legend
Edward Payson (1783-1827)

Published by Solid Ground Christian Books

Special thanks to Iain Murray for permission granted to use
material from his book, *Revival and Revivalism: The Making
and Marring of American Evangelicalism, 1750-1858.*
Published by The Banner of Truth Trust, 1994.

ISBN: 0-9710169-2-5

Cover: Anthony Rotolo Design

Manufactured in the United States of America
1 2 3 4 5 6 7 8 9 10   01 02 03 04 05

Biographical Introduction

Edward Payson started life in 1783 in the parsonage of Rindge in New Hampshire where his father, Seth Payson, had become the Congregational minister twelve months earlier. Payson was a Harvard man. From Harvard he entered the teaching profession at Portland, Maine, but soon answered a call to the ministry and, for the twenty years from 1807 to 1827, served the Second Church of Portland. On his death in 1827 at the age of forty-four a writer likened his earthly path to that of "an angel standing in the sun" (Rev. 19:7), and even those who knew him only from his biography came to understand why he was spoken of as the 'seraphic Payson'. It is a pity that the biography does not also show the more human side of the man who had eight children and invented games for their amusement. But despite its inadequacies, Asa Cummings' memoir of Payson was probably the most influential ministerial biography to appear in the United States in the first half of the nineteenth century.

Like his contemporaries, Edward Dorr Griffin, Lyman Beecher, Asahel Nettleton and Gardiner Spring, Payson enjoyed seasons of refreshing from on high. He was ordained at Portland in 1807, and was noting 'considerable attention to religion' among his people in 1809. Forty-two persons were added to his church in 1810, and much more was to follow in 1814. Preaching in another town in December 1813, he spoke of never having 'seen so much of God's power displayed in the same space of time.' He had to end six days of preaching there in order to return for a church fast and communion at Portland. He wrote to his mother on 7 January 1814, describing what happened on his return:

I came home thoroughly drenched by the shower of divine influences, which began to fall at ----, and soon found that the cloud had followed me, and was beginning to pour itself down upon my people. Instead of a fast, we appointed a season of thanksgiving. A blessing seemed to follow it. I then invited the young men of the parish to come to my house, on Sabbath evening, for religious purposes. The church thought none would come. I expected twenty at most. The first evening forty came; the second, sixty; and the third, seventy. This was the last Sabbath. Six stopped, after the rest were dismissed, to converse more particularly respecting divine things. About thirty persons are known to be seriously inquiring, and there is every appearance that the work is spreading. Meanwhile, I am so ashamed, so rejoiced, and so astonished, to see what God is doing, that I can scarcely get an hour's sleep.

Although in that year and the next there were repeated evidences of God's presence in Payson's congregation at Portland, it was the year 1816 that 'was the most remarkably distinguished for the effusions of the Holy Spirit on his people of any year of his ministry, with the exception of that in which his happy spirit took its flight.'

Payson had completed twenty years in his Portland pulpit when he died in October 1827. Throughout his ministry he witnessed a regular increase of members interspersed with periods of larger, sudden blessing when the numbers multiplied. After 1816 there were further revivals in 1822 and in 1827, the year of his death. Over the period of his ministry the average increase in membership was more than thirty-five a year; in 1827 the figure was seventy-nine.

The impression that is left on those who read the writings of Payson, as of those who heard him, is that the things about which he spoke were great realities in his own life. His life and preaching illustrated the words of the apostle John, 'That which we have seen and heard declare we unto you.' He appeared to men not so much as an eloquent preacher but as a Christian for whom fellowship with God was a living experience. The evidence of his personal papers abundantly confirms the truth of that impression. His work was not his first business. He aimed to live near to Christ. To know him in private was more important than to speak for him before men. He depended on Christ as 'the foundation of every good thought, desire and affection' in order to live and not simply for his public work. 'At times,' wrote Payson, 'God is pleased to admit his children to nearer approaches and more intimate degrees of fellowship with himself and his Son, Jesus Christ.' From diary entries which were never intended to be published we occasionally see something of the experiences that lay behind such words. For example, he wrote on 22 April 1807:

Spent this day in fasting and prayer. At first was stupid; but soon God was pleased to lift up the light of his countenance upon me, and visit me with his free Spirit. O how infinitely glorious and lovely did God in Christ appear! I saw, I felt, that God was mine, and I his, and was unspeakably happy. Now, if ever, I enjoyed communion with God. He shone sweetly upon me, and I reflected back his beams in fervent, admiring, adoring love. Had a most ravishing view of the glories of heaven, of the ineffable delight with which the Lord Jesus beholds the happiness which he has purchased with his own blood.

The secret of the influence of this man was that in his being much with Christ he was indeed the reflector of 'his beams.'

But if it be asked how he attained to being such a close disciple the answer may be surprising. It was not that he had reached some higher ground in the way of holiness. On the contrary, what marked him most was his low view of himself. Payson often noted the pain of his unworthiness and his failure as a Christian. On 18 December 1817 he recorded in his diary: 'Began to think, last night, that I have been sleeping all my days; and this morning felt sure of it... How astonishingly blind have I been, and how imperceptible my religious progress.' Again, in 1821 he told a ministerial friend, 'My parish, as well as my heart, very much resembles the garden of a sluggard; and, what is worse, I find that most of my desires for the melioration of both proceed either from pride, or vanity or indolence.'

Statements such as these show us the nature of the relationship with God that this man had. His felt need lay behind his frequent prayer and his dependence on Christ. Earnestness in prayer, says Payson, requires a true view of oneself: 'You cannot make a rich man beg like a poor man; you cannot make a man that is full cry for food like one who is hungry: no more will a man who has a good opinion of himself cry for mercy like one who feels that he is poor and needy.' This was the heart of Christian experience. A brokenhearted penitent was what this man knew himself to be all his days. He sought to live in the experience of the grace of God to the wholly undeserving and never ceased to pray for the Spirit who shed the love of God abroad in his heart. This was the desire that kept him coming back to him.

It will always be true that the further preachers enter into true evangelical experience, and the more they know of the Spirit of Christ, the more will the elements of tenderness and love, doxology and praise enter into their ministries. Payson entered deeply into this love, and reflected it to an eminent degree. More readers of Payson today would surely bring blessings to the churches.

Iain Murray,
taken from *Revival and Revivalism*

Preface

"He that walketh with wise men shall be wise; but a companion of fools shall be destroyed" (Proverbs 13:20). For many years it has been my deep conviction that these words of the wise man apply to the living and the dead. We have the privilege of walking with wise men who have been long dead by taking up and reading what they wrote. This is one of the great gifts of writing; it permits us to have intimate fellowship with those who lived long before us.

Solid Ground Christian Books is delighted to be able to introduce another wise man from the past. As you can read in Iain Murray's Introduction, Edward Payson was no ordinary man. He was a precious gift from Christ to his church. This small volume is intended as an introduction to this great man. It is hoped that all who read it will be moved to read everything else they can find about him. The church desperately needs to listen to such men.

Lloyd Sprinkle has put us all in his debt for giving us the *The Complete Works of Edward Payson*. The majority of this little book can be found on pages 459-540 of Volume One of his work. It is a treasure of godly wisdom from the heart of man who walked with God.

In addition to the material from volume one, we have collected material to supplement this small work. Appendix One is a paper that was read before the Maine Historical Society by Dr. Cyrus Hamlin, a retired missionary who was privileged to sit under Payson's ministry as a teenager. It is a wonderful testimony. Appendix Two is the entire Ordination Service of Payson that took place on December 16, 1807 in Portland, Maine. His father, Rev. Seth Payson, delivered the Sermon, and two other men from neighboring towns gave the Charge to the Candidate and the Right Hand of Fellowship. The service is precious to read, especially when you consider what Payson became.

Legacy of a Legend is the title we have chosen for this work. Edward Payson was truly a legend in his day.

There is no more proof needed than the fact that hundreds and even thousands named their sons after him in hopes that they would grow to be men like him. A legacy is a special treasure that is left behind for others. The legacy left by this remarkable man is his spiritual wisdom.

This book was first released a few years after the death of Payson. It was a labor of love from his family. In the words of his daughter Louisa,

Soon after the publication of my father's Memoir, the design was formed of preparing a small volume of selections from his remembered conversations, addresses at private meetings, Bible classes, etc. As the material which could be collected in this way proved entirely insufficient, it was thought best to complete the work, as nearly as possible in conformity with the original design, by making extracts from his unpublished discourses; and this has accordingly been done... There has been an endeavor to secure variety in the selections, which are arranged with reference to the progress of a mind, from impenitence and unbelief, through the different stages of conviction, to faith and confirmed hope. None of the extracts have before appeared in print. They are given to the public in the earnest hope, that they may be instrumental in accomplishing the wish so often expressed by their author, that he might 'be permitted to do good with his pen, when his tongue should be silent in death.'

In our day, many are familiar with Edward Payson because he was the father of Elizabeth Prentiss, the author of *Stepping Heavenward*. Although she was not quite nine years old when he died, his life made a profound impact upon her. Her most famous hymn, *More Love to Thee, O Christ*, reflects perfectly the heart desire of her precious father. Her husband stated that 'his memory seemed invested with the triple halo of father, hero and saint. A little picture of him was always near her. She never mentioned his name without tender affection and reverence... What someone said of Sara Coleridge might indeed have been said with no less truth of Elizabeth Payson: "Her father had looked down into her eyes and left in them the light of his own."'

It is a great honor to be able to fulfill the desire of Edward Payson, which he never expected to take place. In response to a request from an association in Boston, for a copy of a sermon, he replied, "It would gratify me exceedingly to comply with the request. There is no honor, no favor, that God can bestow, which I should prize more highly than that of doing good with my pen; of leaving something behind me to speak for Christ when I am silent in the dust. But this honor, He who distributes his gifts to every man as he will, does not see fit to grant me. I must resign the privilege of doing good with the pen to those who are more able." As you will soon see, he undervalued the gift God gave to him. This book will indeed "speak for Christ" as he is "silent in the dust." To God be the glory!

A word about the best way to read the book is in order. It is not an ordinary book. It was not written by the author as a book. Rather, it is treasure from the heart. It will bear fruit only to those who are willing to take the time to ponder deeply each saying. Those in a hurry will never enter into the depths that are here. Take your time. Think about what you read. May it change you forever.

THE PUBLISHER
August 2001

Contents

God 1

Eternity of God 2

Love of God 2

Wisdom of God 3

Duty of Living to the Glory of God 3

How Can Creatures Glorify God? 4

Reverence for God 5

Duty of Loving God 6

Folly of Preferring Creatures to God 7

God the Only Source of Excellence 7

Duty of Submission to the Will of God 8

All Men the Subjects of Christ 11

Sinfulness of Unbelief 12

Conduct of Men Towards Their Maker 13

Language of Those who Neglect the Bible 16

Language of All who Neglect Prayer 17

Reason of God's Forbearance with Sinners 18

Man's Utter Dependence 19

To the Impenitent 20

God Angry with Sinners 21

Motives to Repentance 22

Objections of Sinners Answered 24

The Folly of Rejecting the Gospel 26

Insufficiency of Human Reason 27

Natural Religion 28

Fate of Those who Reject the Gospel 31

The Wicked Like a Troubled Sea 32

Thoughts of God Painful to the Sinner 33

Satan's Armor 33

Grounds of the Sinner's Peace 34

Conscience 35

A Wounded Spirit who can Bear 36

Sinner's Unwillingness to Go to Christ 38

Excuses of the Sinner Answered 39

The Knowledge of Christ Brings Peace 40

The Convinced Sinner Believing in Christ 41

Effects of Conversion 42

The Self-Confident 45
Christians Dissimilar 46
The Christian and Sinner Distinguished 47
Fear and Hope 48
The Law Honored in the Sinner's Salvation 49
Adam Our Representative 51
Christ Our Representative 52
Divine Attributes Fully Satisfied by the Cross of Christ 53
Sinners Pardoned for Christ's Sake 54
God's Perfections Displayed in the Plan of Redemption 55
Condition of the World without a Savior 56
Christ our Example 59
Christ a Teacher 60
Christ, the Beloved Friend 60
Christ's Invitations to the Weary and Oppressed 62
Christ's Displeasure at Sin 63
The Sufferings of Christ 65
Love of Christ 65
Self-Denial of Christ 67
He Shall See the Trail of His Soul 68
Condescension and Love of Christ 69
Compassion and Condescension of Christ 70
The Language of Penitence 71
Joy of Communing with God 73
A Call to Christians in Time of Revival 74
Christians, Members of the Body of Christ 77
The Christian's Consolation 78
Christ Unchangeable 82
Christ a Helper 84
The Bible Entirely Practical 85
Duty of Studying the Bible 86
Prayer 86
Praise 87
The Lord's Supper 88
Relative Duties of Christians 90
Love One Another 92
Universal Law of Benevolence 92
Duties to the Heathen 93
See that Ye Abound in this Grace Also 94

Christ Glorified in His Church 97
Miscellaneous Directions to Christians 98
O Death! Where is Thy Sting? 100
To Ministers of Christ 100
Happiness of Heaven 102
Anecdotes Extracted from a Religious Magazine 104

MATERIAL ADDED TO THE ORIGINAL BOOK

A Letter to His Wife Before Their Marriage 106
A Letter to His Wife After Their Marriage 106
An Example of his Domestic Influence 107
A Letter to his Mother Early in Ministry 108
Personal Resolutions He Adopted 109
His Rule Regarding Pastoral Visits 109
Books He Found Most Useful to His Soul 110
A Fellow Minister's Description of the Power of His Prayers 110
An Address Delivered to Seaman 111
(For the opening of the Portland Marine Bible Society, Oct. 28, 1821)
Scenes from His Sickbed and Deathbed 121
  *The Touching Testimony of Mrs. Payson Describing his Last Days .. 121
  *His Parting Words to His Congregation Gathered Around Him 122
  *His Dying Words to the Young Men of His Congregation 124
  *A Letter Written to His Sister as He Drew Near to Death 125

Appendix One: Testimony of Dr. Cyrus Hamlin 127
(Missionary-Educator, read before the Maine Historical Society)

Appendix Two: The Ordination Service of Edward Payson 135
  *Ordination Discourse by Rev. Seth Payson 136
  *The Charge to the Candidate by Rev. Joseph Buckminster 155
  *The Right Hand of Fellowship by Rev. Caleb Bradley 160

Recommended Reading on Edward Payson 163

GOD

How much this title implies, no tongue, human or angelic, can ever express; no mind conceive. It is a volume of an infinite number of pages, and every page full of meaning. It will be read by saints and angels, through the ages of eternity, but they will never reach the last page, nor fully comprehend the meaning of a single line.

Look back to the time when God existed independent and alone; when there was nothing but God; no heavens, no earth, no angels, no men. How wretched would we, how wretched would any creature be, in such a situation! But Jehovah was then infinitely happy; happy beyond all possibility of increase. He is an overflowing fountain, a bottomless and shoreless ocean of being, perfection, and happiness; and when this infinite ocean overflows, suns and worlds, angels and men, start into existence.

I would ask you to pause and contemplate, for a moment, this wonderful Being. But where shall we stand to take view of him? When we wish to contemplate the ocean, we take our stand upon its shore. But this infinite ocean of being and perfection has no shore. There is no place where we can stand to look at him, for he is in us, around us, above us, below us. Yet, in another sense, there is no place where we may not look at him, for he is everywhere. We see nothing which he has not made, no motion which he does not cause; for he is all, and in all, and above all, God over all, blessed forever. Even he himself cannot tell us fully what he is, for our minds cannot take it in. He can only say to us, "I am that I am. I am Jehovah."

ETERNITY OF GOD

Try, for a moment, to conceive of a Being without a beginning; a Being who does not become older as ages roll away. Fly back, in imagination, millions of millions of millions of years, till reason is confounded, and fancy wearied in the flight. God then existed, and, what may at first appear paradoxical, he had then existed as long as he has now; you would then be no nearer the beginning of his existence than you are now, for it has no beginning, and you cannot approach to that which does not exist. Nor will his being ever come to an end. Add together ages of ages; multiply them by the leaves on the trees, the sand on the seashore, and the dust of the earth, still you will be no nearer the termination of Jehovah's existence, than when you first began your calculation. And let us remember that the duration of his existence is the only measure of our own. As it respects futurity, we are all as immortal as Jehovah himself.

LOVE OF GOD

In the words, "God is love," we have a perfect portrait of the eternal and incomprehensible Jehovah, drawn by his own unerring hand. The mode of expression here adopted, differs materially from that usually employed by the inspired writers, in speaking of the divine perfections. They say, God is merciful, God is just, God is holy; but never do they say, God is mercy, God is justice, God is holiness. In this instance, on the contrary, the apostle, instead of saying, God is loving, or good, or kind, says, God is love, love itself. By this expression we must understand that God is all pure, unmixed love, and that the other moral perfections of his character are only so many modifications of this love. Thus his justice, his mercy, his truth, his faithfulness, are but so many different names of his love or goodness. As the light which proceeds from the sun may easily be separated into many different colors, so the holy love of God, which is the light and glory of his nature, may be separated into a variety of moral attributes and perfections. But, though separated, they are still love. His whole nature and essence are love; his will, his works, and his words, are love; he is nothing, can do nothing but love.

WISDOM OF GOD

Often when the church thinks itself in the most imminent danger, when its friends are ready to cry in despair, "All these things are against us, our destruction is inevitable;" angels are lost in wonder in view of the means which divine wisdom is, even then, employing to effect its deliverance and turn its despondency into triumph. For some thousands of years they have been contemplating this spectacle; their knowledge and their admiration of God's wisdom have been continually increasing, and yet every day they learn something new, every day they see new proofs that Jehovah is indeed the all-wise God; that his resources are inexhaustible; that he can never be at a loss; and that he can effect the same object in numberless different ways, and by the use of the most improbable means.

If the ways of a wise man are above those of a fool, how much more must the ways of the all-wise God exceed ours.

DUTY OF LIVING TO THE GLORY OF GOD

We were created and redeemed for the sole purpose of praising and glorifying our Creator; and if we refuse or neglect to do this, we transgress the great law of creation, frustrate the end of existence, leave unperformed the work for which we were made, and do all in our power to prove that we were created in vain, and to cause God to repent of having made us. Should the sun refuse to shine; should the showers refuse to descend; should the earth refuse to bring forth food; or should trees in a fruitful soil continue barren; would you not say that it was contrary to nature and to the design of their creation; and that since they no longer fulfilled this design, they might properly be reduced to nothing again? And do you not see that while you refuse to praise God, your conduct is equally unnatural, and that you may justly be made the monuments of his everlasting displeasure? What would only be unnatural in inanimate creatures, is the height of folly and wickedness in us; because we are capable of knowing our duty, and are under innumerable obligations to practice it. Let the sun then refuse to shine, the showers to descend, and the earth to be fruitful; but let not rational creatures refuse to praise their Creator, since it is the purpose for which they were created.

HOW CAN CREATURES GLORIFY GOD?

If it be asked how creatures so feeble and ungrateful as we are, can glorify God, I answer, by conducting ourselves in such a manner as naturally tends to make him appear glorious, amiable and excellent in the view of his creatures. A son, for instance, honors his parents, when he evidently loves, reverences, confides in, and obeys them; because such conduct tends to make those who know him think favorably of his parents. A subject honors his sovereign when he cheerfully submits to his authority, and appears to be contented and happy in his government; because this tends to give others a favorable opinion of his sovereign. So men honor and glorify God, when they show by their conduct that they consider him the most perfect and best of beings, and love, reverence and confide in him as such; for these things naturally tend to excite a high estimation of God, in the minds of their fellow creatures.

REVERENCE FOR GOD

With what profound veneration does it become us to enter the presence, and to receive the favors of the awful Majesty of heaven and earth! And how ought we to dread grieving or offending goodness so great, so glorious, so venerable! To illustrate this remark, suppose that the sun, whose brightness, even at this distance, you cannot gaze upon without shrinking, were an animated, intelligent body; and that, with a design to do you good, he should leave his place in the heavens, and gradually approach you. As he drew more and more near, his apparent magnitude and effulgence would every moment increase; he would occupy a larger and larger portion of the visible heavens, until at length all other objects would be lost, and yourselves swallowed up in one insufferably dazzling, overpowering flood of light. Would you not, in such circumstances, feel the strongest emotions of awe, of something like fear? Would a knowledge that the glorious luminary was approaching with a benevolent design for your good, banish these emotions? What, then, ought to be the feelings of a sinful worm of the dust, when the Father of lights, the eternal Sun of the universe, who dwells in the high and holy place, and in the contrite heart, stoops from his awful throne, to visit him, to smile upon him, to pardon him, to purify him from his moral defilement, to adopt him as a child, to make him an heir of heaven, to take possession of his heart as his earthly habitation?

DUTY OF LOVING GOD

We ought to love God because he has given us the power to love. He might have formed us gloomy, morose, misanthropic beings, destitute of all the social affections; without the power of loving any object, and strangers to the happiness of being beloved. Should God withdraw into himself, not only all the amiable qualities which excite love, but the very power of loving, would vanish from the world, and we should not only, like the evil spirits, become perfectly hateful, but should, like them, hate one another.

Every object which can be presented to us has a claim on our affection corresponding to its character. If any object be admirable, it possesses a natural and inherent claim to our admiration; if it be venerable, it has a claim to our reverence; if it be terrible, it demands our fear; if it be beautiful and amiable, it claims and deserves our love. But God is perfectly and infinitely lovely; nay, he is excellence and loveliness itself. If you doubt this, ask those who can tell you. Ask Christ, who is in the bosom of the Father, and he will tell you that God is infinitely lovely. Ask the holy angels, who dwell in his immediate presence, and they will tell you that he is lovely beyond all that even angelic minds can conceive. Ask good men in all ages, and they will lament that they cannot tell you how amiable and excellent Jehovah is. Ask everything beautiful and amiable in the universe, and it will tell you that all its beauty is but a faint reflection of his. If all this does not satisfy you, ask the spirits of disobedience; and they, though filled with malice and rage against him, will tell, if you can constrain them to speak, that the Being they hate is lovely, and that it constitutes the essence of their misery that they can find no blemish in his character. But if God be thus infinitely lovely, we are under infinite obligations to love him; obligations from which he himself cannot release us but by altering his character, and ceasing to be lovely.

FOLLY OF PREFERRING CREATURES TO GOD

Would you not consider a person foolish and absurd, who should extravagantly love and prize a drop of stagnant water, and yet view the ocean with indifference or disgust? or who should constantly grovel in the dust to admire a shining grain of sand, yet neglect to admire the sun which caused it to shine? Of what folly and absurdity, then, are we guilty, when we love the imperfectly amiable qualities of our fellow worms, or admire the sublimity and beauty of the works of nature, and yet exercise no love to him to whom they are indebted for all; him whose glory gilds the heavens, and from whom angels derive everything that can excite admiration or love.

GOD THE ONLY SOURCE OF EXCELLENCE

God only, the Father of lights, from whom cometh down every good and perfect gift, makes one creature to differ from another. They are wise only by his wisdom, strong in his strength, and good in his goodness. He is more entirely the Author of everything good in heaven and on earth, than the sun is the author of that image of himself which is seen in a mirror. When creatures acknowledge this, and ascribe all the excellencies they possess to him alone, they then, in the language of Scripture, bring forth fruit, not to themselves, but to his glory.

God is the source of everything excellent or praiseworthy in the intellectual world. To him angels and men are alike indebted for all their faculties. Reason, memory, wit, prudence, invention and imagination, are only his gifts. The statesman, the warrior, the mathematician, the poet, the orator, the historian, the astronomer, the painter, and the sculptor, all were formed, instructed and directed by him. By his assistance, all the great enterprises, splendid achievements and admirable works which the world ever saw, were performed. "It is he," says David, "who teaches my hands to war, and my fingers to fight." It was he who guided Columbus to the discovery of this new world. It was he who qualified our revered Washington for the great work of delivering his country, and assisted him in its accomplishment. And while we admire the gifts of God in men, shall we not admire the Giver? While we admire the achievements, enterprises and works of men, shall we not admire him who enabled men to perform them? Shall we rest in streams, and admire them only, without praising the fountain? Surely this is highly unreasonable.

DUTY OF SUBMISSION TO THE WILL OF GOD

Suppose that the members of our bodies, instead of being controlled by the will of the head, had each a separate, independent will of its own: would they not, in this case, become useless and even mischievous? Something like this, you are well aware, occasionally takes place. In certain diseases, the members seem to escape from the control of the will, and act as if they were governed by a separate will of their own. When this is the case, terrible consequences often ensue. The teeth shut suddenly and violently, and lacerate the tongue; the elevated hands beat the face and other parts of the body; the feet refuse to support it, and it rolls in the dust a melancholy and frightful spectacle. Such effects we call convulsions. There are convulsions in the moral as well as in the natural world, and they take place when the will of man refuses to be controlled by the will of God. Did all men submit cordially to his will, they would live together in love and harmony, and, like the members of a healthy body, would all promote each other's welfare, and that of the whole system. But they have refused to obey his will, and have set up their own wills in opposition to it; and what has been the consequence? Convulsions, most terrible convulsions, which have, in ten thousand thousand instances, led one member of this great body to injure another; and not only disturbed but almost destroyed the peace of society. What are wars, insurrections, revolutions? What are robberies, piracies, murders, but convulsions in the moral world? convulsions which would never have occurred, had not the will of man refused to submit to the will of God. And never will these convulsions cease, never will universal love, and peace and happiness prevail, until the rebellious will of man shall again submit to the controlling will of God, and his will shall be done on earth as it is in heaven.

If all mankind could be persuaded to say, "Not as I will, but as thou wilt," as sincerely as Christ said it, sin would that moment cease to exist in the world, God and men would be perfectly reconciled, and his will would be done on earth as it is in heaven. Yes, let every human being only say to God, with his whole heart, "Not my will but thine be done," and holiness and happiness would instantly fill the world; men would be embodied angels, and earth would become a sublunary heaven.

I look up to heaven, and there see the blessed and only Potentate, the Creator and Upholder of all things, the infinite and eternal Sovereign of the universe, governing his vast kingdom with uncontrollable power, in a manner perfectly wise, and holy, and just, and good. In this Being I see my Creator, my Preserver, my unwearied Benefactor, to whom I am indebted for everything which I possess. And what does this being see, what has he seen, in me? He sees a frail worm of the dust, who is of yesterday, and knows nothing, who cannot take a single step without making mistakes, who is wholly incompetent to guide himself, and who, by his own folly, is self-destroyed. He has seen this frail, blind, erring worm, presumptuously daring to criticize and censure his proceedings, to interfere in his government of the universe, and to set up his own perverse will against the will of his Creator, his Sovereign, and his God; his own ignorance against divine omniscience, and his own folly against infinite wisdom. This he has seen in me, and this he has seen in you; and who, that believes God has seen this in him, can avoid feeling overwhelmed with sorrow, and shame, and remorse? We may say what we please of the difficulty of repenting, but it would seem to be a thousand fold more difficult to refrain from repenting, after having been guilty of conduct like this. O, then, come and perform this easy, this most reasonable duty. Come, and repent, before God, of your disobedience and opposition to his will, receive through Christ a free and gracious pardon, and then learn of him who was meek and lowly in heart, to say, "Father, not my will, but thine, be done."

Should an angel who knew nothing of our characters, but who had heard of the blessings which God has bestowed on us, visit this world, would he not expect to find every part of it resounding with the praises of God and his love? Would he not expect to hear old and young, parents and children, all blessing God for the glad tidings of the gospel, and crying, "Hosanna to the son of David"? How, then, would he be grieved and disappointed! How astonished to find that Being whom he had ever heard praised in the most rapturous strains by all the bright armies of heaven, slighted, disobeyed, and dishonored, by his creatures on earth! Would you not be ashamed, would you not blush to look such a visitor in the face? to tell him how little you have done for God, tell him that you are not one of his servants? O, then, let us strive to wipe away this foul stain, this disgrace to our race and our world. Let not this world be the only place, except hell, where God is not praised. Let us not be the only creatures, except devils, who refuse to praise him.

ALL MEN THE SUBJECTS OF CHRIST

The subjects of Christ's mediatorial kingdom are divided into two grand classes: those who are obedient, and those who are rebellious. The former class is composed of good men and angels, the latter of wicked men and devils. The former serves Christ willingly and cheerfully. He rules them with the golden scepter of love; his law is written in their hearts; they esteem his yoke easy and his burden light, and habitually execute his will. All the bright armies of heaven, angels and archangels, who excel in strength, are his servants, and go forth at his command, as messengers of love, to minister to the heirs of salvation, or as messengers of wrath to execute vengeance on his enemies. Nor are his obedient subjects to be found only in heaven. In this world, also, the standard of the cross, the banner of his love, is erected, and thousands and millions, who were once his enemies, have been brought willing captives to his feet, have joyfully acknowledged him as their Master and Lord, and sworn allegiance to him as the Author of their salvation. Nor is his authority less absolute over the second class of his subjects, who still persist in their rebellion. In vain do they say, "We will not have this man to reign over us." He rules them with a rod of iron, causes even their wrath to praise him, and makes them the involuntary instruments of carrying on his great designs. He holds all the infernal spirits in a chain, governs the conquerors, monarchs and great ones of the earth, and in all things wherein they deal proudly, he is still above them. In one or the other of these ways, all must serve Christ. Is it not better to serve him willingly, and be rewarded, than to serve him reluctantly, and be destroyed?

SINFULNESS OF UNBELIEF

The reason why persons who appear to be in some measure convinced of sin, so often lose their convictions; and why so many professors of religion fall away and disgrace their profession, is, because the work of conviction was never thoroughly performed; because they were never convinced of unbelief. They saw, perhaps, that they were sinners. They felt convinced of many sins in their tempers and conduct; they in some measure corrected and laid aside these sins; then their consciences ceased to reproach them, and they flattered themselves that they had become new creatures. But, meanwhile, they knew nothing of the great sin of unbelief, and therefore never confessed, repented of, or forsook it, until it proved their destruction. They were like a man who should go to a physician to be healed of some slight external wound, while he knew nothing of a deep-rooted disease which was preying upon his vital organs. Professors of religion, try yourselves by these remarks. Look back to the time when you imagined yourselves to be convinced of sin, and say whether you were then convinced, or whether you have at any time since been convinced of the exceeding sinfulness of unbelief. If not, there is great reason to fear that you are deceived, that you have mistaken the form for the power of godliness.

It is God's invariable method to humble before He exalts; to show us our diseases before He heals them; to convince us that we are sinners before He pronounces our pardon. When, therefore, the Spirit of all grace and consolation comes to comfort and sanctify a sinner, He begins by acting the part of a Reprover, and thus convincing him of sin. The sin of which He more particularly aims to convince him is unbelief. "He shall reprove the world of sin," says our Savior. Why? Because they are murderers, thieves, or adulterers? No. Because they are guilty of slander, fraud, or extortion? No. Because they are intemperate, dissipated, or sensual? No. Because they are envious, malicious, or revengeful? No; but because they are unbelievers, "because they believe not on me" (see John 16:8,9).

If there is one fact, or doctrine, or promise in the Bible, which has produced no practical effect upon your temper or conduct, be assured that you do not truly believe it.

CONDUCT OF MEN TOWARDS THEIR MAKER

Mankind seem to consider God as a sort of outlaw, who has no rights; or, as least, as one whose rights may be disregarded and trampled on at pleasure. They allow that promises made to each other ought to be fulfilled; but they violate, without scruple, those promises which they often make to God, in an hour of seriousness, sickness, or

13

affliction. They allow that earthly rulers ought to be obeyed, but they seem to think that no obedience is due to the Sovereign Ruler of the universe. They allow that children ought to love, honor, and submit to their parents; but they do not appear to think that either love, honor, or submission, should be paid to our Father in heaven. They allow that gratitude is due to human benefactors, and that to requite their favors with ingratitude, is a proof of abominable wickedness; but they practically deny that any grateful return should be made to our heavenly Benefactor for his innumerable benefits, and seem to consider the blackest ingratitude towards him as scarcely a sin.

When a son forsakes his father's house; when he refuses to comply with his entreaties to return; when he chooses to endure all the evils of poverty rather than return, we are ready to suspect that his father must be a very disagreeable, unlovely, or cruel character, since his own children cannot live with him. At least, we shall think this unless we have a very bad opinion of the son. We must condemn one or the other. So, when God's own creatures, whom he has nourished and brought up as children, forsake him, and refuse to return or be reconciled, it gives other beings cause to suspect that he must be a very cruel, unlovely being; and they must either conclude that he is so, or form a very bad opinion of us. Now, sinners will not allow that the fault is theirs; of course they throw all the blame upon their Creator, and represent him as such an unkind, cruel Parent, that his children cannot live with or please him. It is true, God has power to vindicate his own character, and to show the universe that the fault is wholly ours. But this is no thanks to us. The tendency of our conduct is still the same; it still tends to load his character with the blackest infamy and disgrace. This is all the return we make him for giving us existence. Thus do you requite the Lord, O foolish people, and unwise.

"Will a man rob God? Yet you have robbed me" (Malachi 3:8). It is evident that you withhold your hearts from God; or, in other words, rob him of your affections, the very thing which he principally desires. And is this a small offense? Should a person rob you of the affection and esteem of the partner of your bosom, of your children, or your friends, would you not think it a great injury? Would it not in many instances be worse than robbing you of your property? And is it, then, a trifling offense for intelligent creatures to rob their Creator, Father and benefactor, of that supreme place in their affections to which He has a most perfect right, and which He prizes above everything they possess?

The world is, in some form or other, the great Diana, the grand idol of all its inhabitants, so long as they continue in their natural sinful state. They bow down to it; they worship it; they spend and are spent for it; they educate their children in its service; their hearts, their minds, their memories, their imaginations, are full of it; their tongues speak of it; their hands grasp it; their feet pursue it. In a word, it is all in all to them, while they give scarcely a word, a look, or a thought to him who made and preserves them; and who is really all in all. Thus men rob God of their bodies and spirits, which are his, and practically say, "We are our own; who is Lord over us?"

From the manner in which we habitually treat the Bible, we may learn what are our feelings and dispositions towards God; for as we treat the word of God, so should we treat God himself, were he to come and reside among us, in a human form, as he once dwelt on earth in the form of his Son. The contents of Scripture are a perfect transcript of the divine mind. If, then, God should come to dwell among us, he would teach the same things that the Scriptures teach, and pronounce upon us the same sentence which they pronounce. We should therefore feel towards him as we now feel towards them. If we reverence, and love, and obey the Scriptures, then we should reverence, love and obey God. But if we dislike or disbelieve the Scriptures, if we seldom study them, or read them only with indifference and neglect, we should treat God in the same manner. Never would he be a welcome guest in a family where his word is neglected.

LANGUAGE OF THOSE WHO NEGLECT THE BIBLE

No man will ever voluntarily neglect to make himself acquainted with the contents of a message sent to him by one whom he acknowledges as his superior, or on whom he feels himself to be dependent. Let a subject receive a communication from his acknowledged sovereign, and as it claims, so it will receive his immediate attention. Nor will he, especially if it contains various and important instructions, think a hasty perusal of it sufficient. No, he will study it till he feels confident that he is acquainted with its contents, and understands their import. At least equally certain, and equally evident is it, that every man whose heart acknowledges God to be his rightful Sovereign, and who believes that the Scriptures contain a revelation from him, will study them attentively, study them till he feels confident that he understands their contents, and that they have made him wise unto salvation. The man who does not thus study them, who negligently suffers them to lie, for days and weeks, unopened, says, more explicitly than any words can say, "I am Lord; God is not my Sovereign; I am not his subject, nor do I consider it important to know what he requires of me. Carry his messages to those who are subject to him, and they will, perhaps, pay them some attention."

LANGUAGE OF ALL WHO NEGLECT PRAYER

It is natural to man, from his earliest infancy, to cry for relief when in danger or distress, if he supposes that any one able to relieve him is within hearing of his cries. Every man, then, who feels his own dependence upon God, and his need of blessings which God only can bestow, will pray to him. He will feel that prayer is not only his duty, but his highest privilege; a privilege of which he would not consent to be deprived, though confinement in a den of lions were to be the consequence of its exercise. The man, then, who refuses, or neglects to pray, who regards prayer not as a privilege, but as a wearisome and needless task, practically says, in the most unequivocal manner, "I am not dependent on God; I want nothing that he can give; and therefore I will not come to him, nor ask any favor at his hands. I will not ask him to crown my exertions with success, for I am able, and determined, to be the architect of my own fortune. I will not ask him to instruct or guide me, for I am competent to be my own instructor and guide. I will not ask him to strengthen and support me, for I am strong in the vigor and resources of my own mind. I will not request his protection, for I am able to protect myself. I will not implore his pardoning mercy nor his sanctifying grace, for I need, I desire, neither the one nor the other. I will not ask his presence and aid in the hour of death, for I can meet and grapple, unsupported, with the king of terrors, and enter, undaunted and alone, any unknown world into which he may usher me." Such is the language of all who neglect prayer.

REASON OF GOD'S FORBEARANCE WITH SINNERS

How wonderful is the long-suffering and forbearance of God! Here are sinners who have been, for twenty, forty, sixty years, abusing his patience, and misimproving all his benefits. Yet, instead of cutting them down, he adds another year, perhaps many years, to their long since forfeited lives. There are sinners who have wasted and profaned a thousand Sabbaths, yet he allows them another Sabbath, another opportunity of hearing the offers of salvation. There are sinners who have repeatedly been urged in vain to be reconciled to God; yet he condescends still to require a reconciliation. There are sinners at whose hearts Christ has knocked, a thousand and a thousand times; but, though they refuse to admit him, he still knocks again. O, why are such treasures of goodness lavished on such insensible creatures? Why is such an inestimable prize put into the hands of those who have no heart to improve it? Why, indeed, but to show what God can do, and how infinitely his patience and forbearance exceed ours.

One reason why God bestows on sinners the day and the means of grace is, that they may have an opportunity of clearly displaying their own characters, and thus proving the truth of the charges which he has brought against them. He does, as it were, say to the world, "I have accused these creatures of being enemies to me and to all goodness, and of cherishing in their hearts an obstinate attachment to vice. They deny the charge. I am therefore about to bring them to the test; to try an experiment which will clearly show whether my charges are well-founded or not. I shall send them my word, and the gospel of my Son, clearly revealing to them the way of salvation. I shall send messengers to explain and press upon them the truths there revealed. I shall allow them one day in seven to attend on their instructions, and I shall offer them the assistance of my Spirit, to render them holy: these privileges they shall enjoy for years together. If they improve them aright, if they believe my word, receive and love my Son, and renounce their sins, I will acknowledge that I have accused them falsely, that they are not so depraved as I have represented them. But, should they, on the contrary, neglect my word, disbelieve the gospel, and refuse to receive and submit to my Son; should they profane the Sabbath, misimprove the day of grace; refuse to repent of their sins, and be reconciled to me, then it will be evident to all, that I have not accused them falsely; that they are just such depraved, obstinate, irreconcilable enemies to me and to goodness, as I have represented them to be in my word."

MAN'S UTTER DEPENDENCE

If men are truly independent of God, it may, with safety, be asserted, that he is almost the only being or object in the universe, on whom they are not dependent. From the cradle to the grave, their lives exhibit little else than a continued course of dependence. They are dependent on the earth, on the water, on the air, on each other, on irrational animals, on vegetables, on unorganized substances. Let but the sun withhold his beams, and the clouds their showers for a single year, and the whole race of these mighty, independent beings expires. Let but a pestilential blast sweep over them, and they are gone. Let but some imperceptible derangement take place in their frail but complicated frame, and all their boasted intel- lectual powers sink to the level of an idiot's mind. Let a small portion of that food, on which they daily depend for nourishment, pass but the breadth of a line from its proper course, and they expire in agony. An insect, a needle, a thorn, has often proved sufficient to subject them to the same fate. And while they are dependent on so many objects for the continuance of their lives, they are dependent on a still greater number for happiness, and for the success of their enterprises. Let but a single spark fall unheeded, or be wafted by a breath of air, and a city, which it has cost thousands the labors of many years to erect, may be turned to ashes. Let the wind but blow from one point rather than from another, and the hopes of the merchant are dashed against a rock. Let but a little more, or a little less, than the usual quantity of rain descend, and in the latter case the prospects of the husbandman are blasted, while, in the other, his anticipated harvest perishes beneath the clods, or is swept away by an inundation. But in vain do we attempt to describe the extent of man's dependence, or enumerate all the objects and events on which he depends. Yet all these objects and events are under the control of Jehovah. Without his notice and appointment, not a hair falls from our heads, nor a sparrow to the ground. O how far is it, then, from being true, that man is not dependent on God!

TO THE IMPENITENT

My friends, God offers you the water of life, without money and without price. Every one may come and take it if he will; and is not this sufficient? Would you have the water of life forced upon you? What is it that you wish? My friends, I will tell you what you wish. You wish to live as you please here, to disobey your Creator, to neglect your

Savior, to fulfill the desires of the flesh and of the mind; and at death to be admitted into a kind of sensual paradise, where you may taste again the same pleasures which you enjoyed on earth. You wish that God should break his word, stain his justice, purity and truth, and sacrifice the honor of his law, his own rightful authority, and the best interests of the universe, to the gratification of your own sinful propensities.

Look back to those who have passed the great change through which we must all pass. Think of the patriarchs who died before the flood. They have been perfectly happy for more than four thousand years; yet their happiness has but just commenced. Think of the sinners who died before the flood. For more than four thousand years they have been completely wretched, and yet their misery is but begun. So there will be a time when you will have been happy or miserable four thousand years, and for four times four thousand years, and yet your heaven or your hell will even but then be beginning.

GOD ANGRY WITH SINNERS

"God is angry with the wicked every day." Do you ask why he is angry? I answer, He is angry to see rational, immortal, and accountable beings, spending twenty, forty, or sixty years in trifling and sin; serving divers idols, lusts and vanities, and living as if death were an eternal sleep. He is angry to see you forgetting your Maker in childhood, in youth, in manhood, making no returns for all his benefits, casting off his fear, and restraining prayer, and rebelling against him who has nourished and brought you up as children. He is angry to see you laying up treasures on earth, and not in heaven; seeking everything in preference to the one thing needful; loving the praise of men more than the praise of God; and fearing those who can only kill the body, more than him who hath power to cast both soul and body into hell. He is angry to see that you disregard alike his threatenings and his promises; his judgments and his mercies; that you bury in the earth the talents he has given you, and bring forth no fruit to his glory; that you neglect his word, his spirit and his law, and perish in impenitence and unbelief, notwithstanding all the means employed for your conversion. He is angry to see you come before him as his people, and worship him with your lips, while your thoughts are perhaps wandering to the ends of the earth. He is angry to see you trusting in your own wisdom, strength and righteousness for salvation, instead of placing your dependence on Christ, the only name by which you can possibly be saved. These are sins of which every person, in an unconverted state, is guilty; and for these things God is angry, daily angry, greatly and justly angry; and unless his anger be speedily appeased, it will most certainly prove your destruction.

MOTIVES TO REPENTANCE - LUKE 15:10

"God now commandeth all men, everywhere, to repent" (Acts 17:31). I lay this command across your path: you cannot proceed one step farther in a sinful course without treading it under foot. You are urged to the immediate performance of this duty by a regard to your own interest; "for except ye repent, ye shall all likewise perish" (Luke 13:3,5). You are urged to it by all the blessed angels, who are waiting with a desire to rejoice in your conversion. Above all, you are most powerfully urged to it by the blessed Redeemer, whom you are under the strongest possible obligations to love and obey. He has done and suffered much for you. For you he had toiled, bled and died. For you he cheerfully endured the scoffs and cruelties of men; the rage and malice of devils; and the over-whelming weight of his Father's wrath. In return for all this, he asks of you one small favor. He merely requests you to repent and be happy. If you comply with his request, he will see of the travail of his soul, and be satisfied. O, then, be persuaded to give joy to God, to his Son, and to the holy angels; to make this day a festival in heaven, by repenting. Even now, your heavenly Father is waiting for your return, and the Redeemer stands ready with expanded arms to receive you. Even now the white robes and the ring are provided, and the fatted calf is made ready to feast returning prodigals. Even now, angels and archangels are ready to pour forth their most joyful songs to celebrate your return. Will you, then, by persisting in impenitence, seal up their lips? Will you say, there be no joy in heaven, this day, on your account? God shall not be glorified, Christ shall not be gratified, angels shall not rejoice if we can prevent it? If there be any of whose feelings and conduct this is the language, I solemnly, but reluctantly declare unto you, in the name of Jehovah, that God and his Son shall be glorified, and there shall be joy over you in heaven, notwithstanding all your endeavors to prevent it. Never shall any of his creatures rob God of his glory; and, if you will not consent that his grace shall be glorified in your salvation, he will be compelled to glorify his justice, in your everlasting destruction. If you will not allow the inhabitants of heaven to rejoice in your repentance, their love of justice, truth and holiness will constrain them to rejoice in your condemnation, and to sing, "Alleluia," while the smoke of your torment ascendeth up forever and ever (Rev. 19:3).

OBJECTIONS OF SINNERS ANSWERED

Suppose that, while you are dying of a fatal disease, a medicine of great reputed efficacy is offered you, on making trial of which, you find yourself restored to health and activity. Full of joy and gratitude, you propose the remedy to others, afflicted with the same disease. One of these persons replies to you, "I am surprised that you place so much faith in the virtues of this medicine. How do you know that it was really discovered by the person whose name it bears? Or, even if it were, it is so many years ago, and the medicine has passed through so many hands since, that it is probably corrupted, or perhaps some other has been substituted in the place of the genuine medicine." Says another, "It may not be suited to the constitutions of men in this age, though it was undoubtedly useful to those who first used it." "The disease and the cure are both equally imaginary," says a third. "There are many other remedies of equal or superior efficacy," objects a fourth. "None of the most celebrated physicians recommend it," replies a fifth; while a sixth attempts to silence you by objecting to the bottles in which it is put up, and repeating that boxes would have been more suitable. What weight would all these objections have with you? Would they induce you to throw away the healing balm, whose effects you even then felt, sending life, and health, and vigor, through your whole frame? Even thus may infidels and cavillers urge objections against the gospel; but the genuine Christian heeds them not, for he has felt, in his own soul, its life-giving power.

Will you say there are no real stars, because you see meteors fall, which for a time appeared to be stars? Will you say that blossoms never produce fruit, because many of them fall off, and some fruit, which appears sound, is rotten at the core? Equally absurd is it to say there is no such thing as real religion, because many who profess it fall away, or prove to be hypocrites in heart. Or will you say that a medicine does no good, because, though it removes the fever, it does not restore the patient to perfect strength in an instant? Equally groundless and absurd is it to say that religion does not make its possessor better, because it does not, in a moment, make them perfect as the angels of God.

The many false and counterfeit appearances which we meet with, instead of proving that there is no religion in the world, not only prove that there is, but that it is extremely precious; otherwise it would not be counterfeited. No one will be at the trouble of counterfeiting, either what does not exist, or what is of no value. No one will make false stones, or false dust, though many make false pearls and diamonds. If there were no real money, there would be no counterfeit; and so, if there were no real religion, there would be no false religion. One cannot exist without the other any more than a shadow can exist without a substance; and he who rejects all religion, because hypocrites sometimes borrow its name and appearance, acts no less absurdly than he who throws his gold or jewels into the fire, because gold and jewels have sometimes been counterfeited.

Surely, if Christianity be a delusion, it is a blessed delusion indeed; and he who attempts to destroy it is an enemy to mankind. It is a delusion which teaches us to do justly, love mercy, and walk humbly with our God (Micah 6:8); and delusion which teaches us to love our Maker supremely, and our neighbor as ourselves; a delusion which bids us love, forgive, and pray for our enemies, render good for evil, and promote the glory of God and the happiness of our fellow creatures, by every means in our power; a delusion, which, wherever it is received, produces a humble, meek, charitable and peaceful temper, and which, did it universally prevail, would banish wars, vice and misery from the world. It is a delusion which not only supports and comforts its believers in their wearisome progress through this vale of tears, but attends them in death, when all other consolations fail, and enables them to triumph over sorrows, sickness, anguish and the grave. If delusion can do this, in delusion let me live and die; for what could the most blessed reality do more?

FOLLY OF REJECTING THE GOSPEL.

Shall we listen to men when God speaks? Shall blind and ignorant worms of the dust pretend to know what God will do, better than he who was from eternity in the bosom of the Father? Hast thou, O man, whosoever thou art, that pretendest that the words of Christ are unreasonable, or improbable, or false, hast thou ascended into heaven, or descended into hell? Hast thou measured eternity and grasped infinity? Hast thou by searching found out God? Hast thou found out the Almighty unto perfection? Canst thou tell me more of him than can the Son of his love, in whom are hid all the treasures of wisdom and knowledge? Does the dim candle of thy darkened reason shine brighter than the glorious Sun of righteousness? And are those to be branded as fools and madmen, who choose to walk in his light, rather than to be led by a mere will of the wisp? No; till you can bring us a teacher superior to Christ, who is the wisdom of God; till you can show us a man who has weighed the mountains in the hollow of his hand, and meted out heaven with a span; who has lived in heaven from eternity; and can prove that he knows more than Omniscience; we will, we must cleave to Christ. Here is a rock. All is sea besides. Nor shall the unbelief of sinners make the faith of God without effect; for, if we believe not, he remains faithful; he cannot deny himself.

INSUFFICIENCY OF HUMAN REASON

Viewed through any other medium than that of revelation, man is a riddle which man cannot expound; a being composed of inconsistencies and contradictions, which unassisted reason must forever seek in vain to reconcile. In vain does she endeavor to ascertain the origin, object and end of his existence. In vain does she inquire in what his duty and happiness consist. In vain does she ask what is his present concern and future destination. Wherever she turns for information, she is soon lost in a labyrinth of doubts and perplexities, and finds the progress of her researches interrupted by a cloud of obscurity which the rays of her feeble lamp are insufficient to penetrate.

Suppose you should see a man carrying a little, glimmering candle in his hand at noonday, with his back turned to the sun, and foolishly endeavoring to persuade himself and others that he had no need of the sun, and that his little candle gave more light than that glorious luminary. How amazingly great would be his folly! Yet this illustration very feebly represents the folly of those who walk in the sparks of their own kindling, while they disregard the glorious Sun of righteousness (see Isaiah 50:11).

NATURAL RELIGION

I know that those who hate and despise the religion of Jesus because it condemns their evil deeds, have endeavored to deprive him of the honor of communicating to mankind the glad tidings of life and immortality; I know that they have dragged the moldering carcass of paganism from the grave, animated her lifeless form with a spark stolen from the sacred altar, arrayed her in the spoils of Christianity, re-enlightened her extinguished candle at the torch of revelation, dignified her with the name of natural religion, and exalted her in the temple of reason, as a goddess, able, without divine assistance, to guide mankind to truth and happiness. But we also know, that all her boasted pretensions are vain, the offspring of ignorance, wickedness and pride. We know that she is indebted to that revelation which she presumes to ridicule and condemn, for every semblance of truth or energy which she displays. We know that the most she can do, is to find men blind and leave them so; and to lead them still farther astray, in a labyrinth of vice, delusion and wretchedness. This is incontrovertibly evident, both from past and present experience; and we may defy her most eloquent advocates to produce a single instance, in which she has enlightened or reformed mankind. If, as is often asserted, she is able to guide us in the path of truth and happiness, why has she ever suffered her votaries to remain a prey to vice and ignorance? Why did she not teach the learned Egyptians to abstain from worshipping their leeks and onions? Why not instruct the polished Greeks to renounce their sixty thousand gods? Why not persuade the enlightened Romans to abstain from adoring their deified murderers? Why not prevail on the wealthy Phoenicians to refrain from sacrificing their infants to Saturn? Or, if it was a task beyond her power to enlighten the ignorant multitude, reform their barbarous and abominable superstitions, and teach them that that were immortal beings, why did she not, at least, instruct their philosophers in the great doctrine of the immortality of the soul, which they earnestly labored in vain to discover? They enjoyed the light of reason and natural religion, in its fullest extent; yet so far were they from ascertaining the nature of our future and eternal existence, that they could not determine whether we should exist at all beyond the grave; nor could all their advantages preserve them from the grossest errors and most unnatural crimes.

What would you say of a man who should throw away his compass, because he could not tell why it points to the north? or reject an accurate chart, because it did not include a delineation of coasts which he never expected to visit, and with which he had no concern? What would you say of a man who should reject all the best astronomical treatises, because they do not describe the inhabitants of the moon, and of the planets; or who should treat with contempt every book which does not answer all the questions that may be asked respecting the subject of which it treats? Or, to come still nearer to the point, what would you say of a man, who, when sick of a mortal disease, should refuse an infallible remedy, unless the physician would first tell him how he took the disease, how such diseases first entered the world, why they were permitted to enter it, and by what secret laws or virtues the offered remedy would effect his cure? Would you not say, a man so unreasonable deserves to die? He must be left to suffer for his folly. Now, this is precisely the case of those who neglect the Bible because it does not reveal those secret things which belong to God (Deut. 29:29). Your souls are assailed by fatal diseases, by diseases which have destroyed millions of your fellow creatures, which already occasion you much suffering, and which, you are assured, will terminate in death unless removed. An infallible Physician is revealed to you in the Bible, who has, at a great expense, provided a certain remedy; and this remedy He offers you freely, without money and without price. But you refuse to take this remedy, because He does not think it necessary to answer every question which can be asked respecting the origin of your disease, the introduction of such diseases into the world, and the reasons why they were ever permitted to enter it. Tell me, you exclaim, how I became sick, or I will not consent to be well. If this be not the height of folly and madness, what is?

We have not the smallest reason to suppose that, if God had revealed all those secret things which belong to him, it would have made it more easy than it is now, to know and perform our duty. Suppose, for instance, that God should answer all the questions which may be asked respecting the origin of moral evil, and its introduction into the world; would this knowledge at all assist us in banishing evil from the world, or from our own bosoms? As well might we pretend that a knowledge of the precise manner in which a man was killed would enable us to restore him to life. Or, should God inform us of the manner in which divinity and humanity are united in the person of Jesus Christ, would this knowledge assist us in performing any one of the duties we owe the Savior? As well might we pretend that a knowledge of the manner in which our souls are united to our bodies, would assist us in performing any of the common actions of life.

The Bible tells us that an enemy came and sowed tares. Now, if any man chooses to go farther than this, and inquire where the enemy got the tares, he is welcome to do so; but I choose to leave it where the Bible leaves it. I do not wish to be wise above what is written.

FATE OF THOSE WHO REJECT THE GOSPEL

It is God's invariable rule of proceeding to deal with his creatures, in some measure, as they deal with him. Hence we are told that, with the upright, he will show himself upright; with the merciful, he will show himself merciful; and with the froward, he will show himself froward (Psalm 18:25,26). When, therefore, persons come to him with a pretended desire to know their duty, but, in reality, with a view to find some excuse or justification for their errors and sins, he will suffer them, as a punishment, to find something which will harden them in their wickedness. Thus he will suffer the obstinate believer in universal salvation, to deceive himself with his delusive dreams, till he wakes in torments. He will suffer the proud, self-righteous opposer of his gospel, to trust in his moral duties, till it is too late to discover his mistake. He will suffer the self-deceived hypocrite to please himself with his false hopes of heaven, till he finds the door forever shut against him. All these persons did, in effect, wish to be deceived; they hated the light, shut their eyes, and would not come to it; they leaned to their own understandings, instead of trusting to the Lord; they never prayed him to keep them from self-deception and from false paths; they chose to believe Satan rather than God, and therefore are justly left to feel the effects of it.

THE WICKED, LIKE A TROUBLED SEA

Ungoverned passions are to the mind what winds are to the ocean, and they often throw it into a storm; for, in such a world as this, the sinner must meet with many things which are calculated to rouse them. Sometimes he is injured, injured perhaps without cause or provocation; and then his mind is agitated by revengeful feelings. Sometimes he sees a rival, perhaps an unworthy rival, outstrip him in the race, and seize the prize which he had hoped to obtain; and, in consequence, envy, mortification, and chagrin, lie gnawing at his heart, and cause the greater pain because he is obliged to conceal them. Often he meets with some slight affront or insult, which wounds his pride, and sets his angry passions in a flame, like Haman, who could enjoy nothing because Mordecai refused to do him reverence. In addition to these things, he is daily exposed to a thousand little nameless vexatious occurrences, which tease, and fret, and harass him, rendering his mind a stranger to peace. Often, too, his mind is disturbed by its own workings, without any assignable cause. He feels restless and unhappy, he can scarcely tell why. He wants something, but he cannot tell what. One wave of troubled thought after another, comes rolling upon his mind, and he cannot say with the Psalmist, "In the multitude of my thoughts within me, thy comforts delight my soul" (Ps. 94:19). These troublesome thoughts, and tumultuous workings of the mind, are to the wicked man what the daily flow and ebb of the tide are to the ocean. They keep it in agitation even when the waves of passion cease to flow.

THOUGHTS OF GOD PAINFUL TO THE SINNER

Sinners do not like to retain God in their knowledge, because He is omniscient and omnipresent. In consequence of his possessing these attributes, he is a constant witness of their feelings and conduct, and is perfectly acquainted with their hearts. This must render the thoughts of his holiness still more disagreeable to a sinner, for what can be more unpleasant to such a character, than the constant presence and inspection of a holy being, whom he cannot deceive, from whose keen, searching gaze he cannot for a moment hide, to whom darkness and light are alike open, and who views the sinner's conduct with the utmost displeasure and abhorrence? Even the presence of our fellow creatures is disagreeable, when we wish to indulge any sinful propensity which they will disapprove. The slanderer, the profane swearer, the drunkard, the debauchee and the gamester would feel the presence of a religious inferior to be irksome, though he should be present but for an hour. How exceedingly irksome, then, must the constant presence of a holy, heart-searching God be to a sinner! But if the sinner retains a knowledge of God, he must feel him to be present. No wonder, then, that sinners banish a knowledge of him from their minds, as the easiest method of freeing themselves from the restraint imposed by his presence.

SATAN'S ARMOR

The armor with which Satan furnishes his followers, is directly the reverse of that Christian armor described by the apostle Paul (Ephesians 6:11-18). Instead of a girdle of truth, he girds the sinner with the girdle of error and deceit. Instead of the breastplate of Christ's righteousness, he furnishes him with a breastplate of his own fancied righteousness. Instead of the shield of faith, the sinner has the shield of unbelief; and with this he defends himself against the curses of the law, and the arrows of conviction. Instead of the sword of the Spirit, which is the word of God, he teaches them to wield the sword of a tongue set on fire of hell, and furnishes them with a magazine them with a magazine of cavils, excuses, and objections, with which they attack religion, and defend themselves. He also builds for them many refuges of lies, in which, as in a strong castle, they proudly hope to shelter themselves from the wrath of God.

The false peace and security in which sinners indulge, instead of proving their safety, is only a further evidence of their danger. It proves that the strong man armed is not disturbed in his possessions, but he keeps them in peace.

GROUNDS OF THE SINNER'S PEACE

There is, perhaps, scarcely a person to be found, who does not, in his own opinion, exemplarily perform some part of his duty. On this he looks with no small degree of self-complacency, and flatters himself that it will atone for all obliquities in his temper and conduct. To this he flies for refuge whenever conscience reproves his deficiencies, and, instead of believing the apostolic assertion, that if a man shall keep the whole law, and yet offend in one point, he is guilty of all, seems to suppose that if he transgresses the whole law, and yet obeys one precept, he is guiltless. I have met with a person who, though guilty of almost every crime which could disgrace her sex, thanked God, with much apparent self-gratulation, that she was not a thief;

and who evidently imagined that her abstaining from this one vice would secure her from the displeasure of heaven.

CONSCIENCE

Conscience is God's vice-regent in the soul, and thought sinners may stupefy and sear, they cannot entirely silence or destroy it. At times, this unwelcome monitor will awake, and then her reproaches and threatenings are, above all things, terrible to the sinner. During the day, while he is surrounded by thoughtless companions, or wholly engrossed by worldly pursuits, he may contrive to stifle, or at least to disregard, her voice; but at night, and upon his bed, when all is silent around him, when darkness and solitude compel him to attend to his own reflections, the case is different. Then an awakened conscience will be heard. Then she arraigns the sinner at her bar, tries, convicts, and condemns him, and threatens him with the punishment which his sins deserve. In vain does he endeavor to fly from her torturing scourge, or to find refuge in sleep. Sleep flies from him. One sin after another rises to his view, and the load of conscious guilt, which oppresses him, becomes more and more heavy, till, like the impious Belshazzar, when he saw the mysterious handwriting upon the wall, the joints of his loins are loosed, and his knees smite one against the other (Daniel 5:1-6). He finds that something must be done. He has heard that prayer is a duty, and he attempts to pray. He utters a few half-formed cries for mercy, makes a few insincere resolutions, and promises of amendment; and having thus, in some measure, quieted the reproaches of his conscience, he falls asleep. In the morning he wakes, happy to see once more the cheerful light; the resolutions and promises of the night are forgotten, he again spends the day in folly and sin, and at night retires to his bed, again to be scourged by conscience for breaking his resolutions, again to quiet her reproaches by insincere prayers and promises, and again to break these promises when the light of day returns.

There is a season, and often, perhaps, more than one, in the life of almost every person who hears the gospel faithfully preached, in which it affects him more than ordinarily. Something like light appears to shine into his mind, which enables him to discover objects previously unseen or unnoticed. While this light continues to shine, he feels a much more full and strong conviction of the truth of the Bible, and of the reality and importance of religion, than he ever felt before. He sees, with more or less clearness, that he is a sinner; that, as such, he is exposed to God's displeasure; and that, unless some means can be found to avert that displeasure, he is undone. After such means, he is, therefore, very inquisitive. He reads the Bible more frequently and carefully, becomes a more diligent, attentive and interested hearer of the gospel, is fond of conversing on religious subjects, and perhaps attempts to pray for mercy. Christ stands at the door of his heart, and knocks for admittance. With a person in this situation, he is as really, though not as visibly, present, as he was with the Jews, when he said, "Yet a little while is the light with you" (John 12:35).

A WOUNDED SPIRIT, WHO CAN BEAR?

One reason why the anguish of a wounded spirit is more intolerable than any other species of suffering, is, that it is impossible to obtain the smallest consolation or relief under it. This can scarcely be said, with truth, of any other species of suffering to which mankind are liable. If they lose friends, they have usually other friends to sympathize with them, and assist in repairing their loss. If they lose property, they may hope to regain it, or, if not, their losses cannot be always present to their mind, and many sources of enjoyment are still open to them. If they are afflicted with painful diseases, they can usually obtain, at least, temporary relief from medicine, and receive some consolation from the sympathy of their friends. In all cases, they can, for a time, lose their sorrows in sleep, and look forward to death as the termination of their troubles. But very different is the situation of one who suffers the anguish of a wounded spirit. He cannot fly from his misery, for it is within. Nor can he forget it, for it is every moment present to his mind. Nor can he divert his attention from it, for it engages his thoughts, in defiance of all endeavors to fix them on any other objects. Nor can he derive consolation from any friends or temporal blessings he may possess, for everything is turned to poison and bitterness, and the very power of enjoyment seems to be taken from him. Nor can he even lose his sorrows in sleep, for sleep usually flies from a wounded spirit, or, if obtained, it is disturbed and unrefreshing. Hence the exclamation of Job, "When I say, My bed shall comfort me, my couch shall ease my complaint; then, thou scarest me with dreams, and terrifiest me through visions" (Job 7:13,14).

Look which way it will for relief, the wounded spirit can discover nothing but aggravations of its wretchedness. If it looks within, it finds nothing but darkness, and tempest and despair. If it looks around on its temporal possessions, it sees nothing but gifts of God which it has abused, and for its abuse of which it must give a terrible account. If it looks back, it sees a life spent in neglect of God, and ten thousand sins, following it as accusers to the judgment seat. If it looks forward, it sees that judgment seat to which it must come, and where it expects nothing but a sentence of final condemnation. If it looks up, it sees that God who is wounding it, and whose anger seems to search it like fire; and if it looks downward, it sees the gulf which awaits its fall. Not even to death can it look forward as the termination of its miseries, for it fears that its miseries will then receive a terrible increase. True, there is one object to which it might look for relief, and find it. It might look to the Savior, the great Physician, and obtain not only a cure for its wounds, but everlasting life. But to him it will not look, till its impenitence and unbelief are subdued by sovereign grace.

SINNER'S UNWILLINGNESS TO GO TO CHRIST

The sinner tries every place of refuge before he will enter the ark of safety. He is like a person exposed to the storm and tempest, for whom a place of safety is provided, which he is unwilling to enter. He flies from one place of fancied security to take refuge in another. The storm increases; one hiding place after another is swept away, till, at length, exposed, without a shelter, to the raging storm, he is glad to flee to the refuge provided for him.

Suppose an apparently strong and healthy man should apply to you for relief, and, when asked why he did not labor for his subsistence, should reply, Because I can find no one to employ me. If you wished to know whether this or indolence were the true reason, you would offer him employment; and if he then refused to labor, you would feel satisfied that he was slothful and undeserving of your charity. So, when God puts into the hands of sinners a price to get wisdom, and they do not improve it, it becomes evident that they do not wish, that they are not willing, to become religious.

EXCUSES OF THE SINNER ANSWERED

Numerous as are the excuses which sinners make when urged to embrace the gospel, they may all be reduced to three; the first is, that they have no time to attend to religion; the second is, that they do not know how to become religious; and the third, that they are not able to become so. Want of time, want of knowledge, or want of power, is pleaded by all. Foreseeing that they would make these excuses, God determined that they should have no reason to make them. By giving them the Sabbath, he has allowed them time for religion. By giving them his word, and messengers to explain it, he has taken away the excuse of ignorance; and by offering them the assistance of his Holy Spirit, he has deprived them of the pretense that they are unable to obey him. Thus he has obviated all their excuses; and therefore, at the last day, every mouth will be stopped, and the whole impenitent world will stand guilty and self-condemned before God.

The convinced sinner wishes to be saved; but then he would be his own savior. He will not consent to be saved by Christ. He cannot bear to come as a poor, miserable, self-condemned sinner, and throw himself on the mere mercy of Christ; but he wants to purchase heaven; to give so many good deeds, as he calls them, for so much happiness hereafter. He goes on to multiply his religious duties, and, with great diligence, makes a robe of his own righteousness, with which he hopes to cover his moral nakedness, and render himself acceptable in the sight of God. In vain is he told that all his righteousness is as filthy rags; that he is daily growing worse, rather than better; that eternal life can never be purchased. He will stop here, as thousands have done before, resting on this foundation, having the form of Godliness, but denying the power, unless the Spirit of God continue to strive with him, and complete the work by showing him his own heart.

THE KNOWLEDGE OF CHRIST BRINGS PEACE

Even a knowledge of the divine perfections, if it could have been obtained without Christ, would only have driven us to despair, as it did our guilty first parents; for outside of Christ, God is a consuming fire. The convinced sinner looks at the greatness of God, and says, "How can he stoop to notice a being so insignificant as myself?" He looks at his holiness, and says, "God cannot but hate me as a vile, polluted sinner." He looks at his justice, and says, "God must condemn me, for I have broken His righteous law." He looks at his truth, and cries, "God is not a man that He should lie; He must execute His threatenings and destroy me." He looks at God's immutability, and says, "He is in one mind, and who can turn him? He will never change; He will always be my enemy." He looks at his power and wisdom, and says, "I can neither resist nor deceive him." He looks at his eternity and exclaims, "It is a fearful thing to fall into the hands of the living God." Thus do all the divine perfections become so many sources of terror and dismay to the convinced sinner. But no sooner does he obtain a knowledge of Christ, than his fears vanish. The divine perfections no longer forbid him to hope for mercy, but encourage him to do it. Instead of the thunders of the law, he hears the compassionate voice of Christ saying, "Be of good cheer, my blood cleanses from all sin; your sins, which are many, are forgiven." He feels boldness to enter into the holiest of all through the blood of Jesus, and exclaims with the apostle, "Being justified by faith, we have peace with God through our Lord Jesus Christ" (Rom. 5:1). Such are the blessed effects which St. Paul experienced from a knowledge of Christ, and which every true believer experiences. Can we then wonder, that, in comparison with it, they count all things but loss.

THE CONVINCED SINNER BELIEVING IN CHRIST

When a convinced, guilty sinner, who feels condemned by the law of God and his own conscience, and fears the sentence of eternal condemnation from the mouth of his Judge hereafter, hears and believes the glad tidings of salvation, they cause hope in the mercy of God to spring up in his anxious, troubled breast. He says to himself, "I am a miserable, guilty creature. I have rebelled against my Creator, broken his law, and thus exposed myself to its dreadful curse. How, then, can I escape from this curse, which threatens to plunge me in eternal ruin? Can I call back the idle words I have uttered, the sinful desires I have indulged, the wicked actions I have committed, the time I have wasted, the precious privileges and opportunities I have misimproved? No. Can I wash away the guilt of these sins from my troubled conscience, or blot out the black catalogue of them which is written in the book of God's remembrance? No. Can I make any satisfaction or atonement for them, to appease my justly-offended God? No. Even should I be perfectly obedient in the future, still this will not blot out my past sins. Besides, I find that I daily commit new sins; so that, instead of diminishing, I increase my guilt. What, then, can I do? Where can I turn?

On what can I build any hope of mercy? Why should God pardon me, and give me heaven, when I have done, and still do nothing but provoke him! What can I, what must I do to be saved? The gospel indeed says, 'Believe on the Lord Jesus Christ, and thou shalt be saved.' It tells me that though my sins be of a crimson color and scarlet dye, yet if I forsake them, and turn unto the Lord, he will abundantly pardon. Why should not I believe in Christ, as well as others? His blood cleanseth from all sin. But perhaps I am too great a sinner to be saved. Yet the gospel assures me that Christ came to save the chief of sinners. Why, then, should I doubt? Why should I not believe? I must, I will, I can, I do believe; Lord, help thou mine unbelief."

EFFECTS OF CONVERSION

When a man stands with his back to the sun, his own shadow and the shadows of surrounding objects are before him. But when he turns towards the sun, all these shadows are behind him. It is the same in spiritual things. God is the great Sun of the universe. Compared with him, creatures are but shadows. But while men stand with their backs to God, all these shadows are before them, and engross their affections, desires and exertions. On the contrary, when they are converted, and turn to God, all these shadows are thrown behind them, and God becomes all in all, so that they can say from the heart, "Whom have we in heaven but thee? and there is none on earth that we desire besides thee" (Psalm 73:25).

The effect produced on a sinner who is brought from darkness into God's marvelous light, may be illustrated in the following manner. The Scriptures teach us that angels are continually present in our world, and employed in executing the designs of God. Being spirits, they are of course invisible to mortal eyes. Hence we are unconscious of their presence, and, therefore are not affected by it. Now, suppose, for the supposition involves no impossibility, that God should impart to anyone of our race the power of seeing these active and benevolent spirits. It is evident that this power would occasion a great change in the conduct and feelings of that man. He would see angels, where other persons could see nothing. He would be interested by the sight; he would wish to form an acquaintance with these newly-discovered beings; he would frequently speak of them, of their employments and pursuits. Of course he would no longer be like other men; he would become, in one sense, a new creature, and the angels would appear to him so much more interesting than other objects, that his attention would be much diverted. Hence he would be thought a visionary or a distracted man. Now, the light of divine truth does not make angels visible, but it makes the Lord of angels, the Father of spirits, in some sense, visible; it makes him, at least, a reality to the mind, or, in the language of Scripture, it enables men to feel and act as if they saw Him who is invisible. It brings God into the circle of objects by which we perceive ourselves to be surrounded; and in whatever circle he is seen, he will be seen to be the most important object in it. Now, if the sight of angels would affect a change in a man's character, much more will seeing the infinite God. His favor will appear all important, his anger dreadful; all other objects will, in a measure, lose their interest, and the man will be thought deluded, or visionary or distracted.

Suppose a man engaged in some enterprise, for the success of which he is exceedingly desirous. He is surrounded, we will suppose, by a number of persons who have it in their power, either to aid or oppose his designs. Knowing this, he will of course, make it his great object to secure their cooperation; or, at least, to induce them not to oppose him. Now, suppose another person to be introduced into the circle around him, possessed of far greater power than any or all of these united, to aid or oppose his designs. This circumstance will produce a great alteration in his views and feelings. It will now be his great object to secure the assistance of this new and more powerful personage; and if he can obtain this, he will neither desire the aid nor fear the opposition of others. To apply this to the case of a sinner, living without God, in the world. He desires to be happy, and, for this purpose, to obtain those worldly objects which he deems necessary to happiness. He finds himself surrounded by creatures, who have power either to aid or oppose him in procuring these objects. Of course, his principal aim is, to avoid their opposition, and secure their friendship and assistance. Now, suppose this man to begin to realize that there is a God; a being who superintends, directs, and governs all creatures and events; who can make him happy without their assistance, or render him miserable, in defiance of all their endeavors to prevent it. Will not the introduction of such a being into the circle around him, produce a great alteration in his plans, his views, and feelings? Before this, he regarded creatures as everything. Now, they will appear comparatively as nothing. Before, God was nothing to him. Now he will be all in all.

The repentant sinner is willing to lie at God's feet, and confess his sins, without even wishing to excuse them.

THE SELF-CONFIDENT

We see many who bid high, and seem to promise fair for heaven. They set out as if they would carry all before them, and say to Christ's people as Orpah did to her mother-in-law, "Surely we will go with you" (Ruth 1:10). For a time they appear to run well. Like a flower plucked from its stalk, and placed in water, they look fair and flourishing. Many of their sins seem to be subdued, and many moral and religious duties are diligently practiced. But at length a day of trial comes. Temptations assault them; the world opposes them; the sins which seemed to be dead revive; the effect of novelty wears off; the tumult of their feelings subsides; their little stock of zeal, and strength, and resolution, is exhausted; and they have never learned to apply to Christ for fresh supplies. Then it appears that they had no root in themselves. They begin to wither. Their blossoms fall off without producing fruit. They first grow weary, then faint, then utterly fall.

He depended on himself, and not on Christ; on his own promises and resolutions, and not on God's. Hence, when his own stock fails, as fail it must, he has nothing. Every one knows that no stream can rise higher than its fountain head. It is the same in religion; the stream that is to rise as high as heaven, must have its fountain head in heaven. It must flow from the river of life which issues out of the throne of God and the Lamb, and from that river it must be fed, or it will dry up.

If, with a careful and enlightened eye, we trace the path of a numerous church, we shall find it strewed with the fallen, the fainting, the slumbering, and the dead, who set out in their own strength, and have been stopped, ensnared and overthrown, by various obstacles and enemies.

CHRISTIANS DISSIMILAR

We must not expect that all persons will see the truths of religion with equal distinctions, or feel an equal degree of joy, on being first brought from darkness into God's marvelous light. While some pass in a moment from the deepest distress and anguish, to the most rapturous emotions of joy and gratitude, others are introduced so gradually into the kingdom, that they are hardly able to tell when they entered it. The subject may be illustrated by the different views and emotions which would be excited in three blind persons, of whom one should be restored to sight at midnight, another at dawn, and the third amid the splendors of the meridian sun. The first, although his sight might be as perfectly restored as that of the others, would yet doubt, for some time, whether any change had been effected in him, and tremble, lest the faint outlines of the objects around him which he so indistinctly discovered, should prove to be the creations of his own fancy. The second, although he might, at first, feel almost assured of the change which had been wrought upon him, would yet experience a gradually-increasing confidence and hope as the light brightened around him, while the third, upon whose surprised and dazzled vision burst at once the refulgence of midday, would be transported, bewildered, and almost overwhelmed, with the excess of surprise, and joy, and gratitude.

THE CHRISTIAN AND SINNER DISTINGUISHED

Suppose you have a child who frequently disobeys your commands, and neglects the duties which you require of him, yet, if this neglect and disobedience seem to proceed from thoughtlessness, rather than from a rebellious disposition; if he appears sincerely penitent, and every day comes and tells you, with tears in his eyes, "Father, I love you; I am sorry that I have done wrong; I am ashamed of myself, and wonder that you have patience to bear with me, and that you do not disinherit me;" you would love and forgive such a child, and feel that there was hope of his reformation. But should your child say, or could you read the feeling in his heart, "Father, I cannot love you; I have never felt one emotion of love towards you; and I have no wish to obey your commands;" would you not say, his case is hopeless; there is nothing for me to work upon; no feeling, no affection, no desire to do right.

Suppose you wished to separate a quantity of brass and steel filings, mixed together in one vessel, how would you effect this separation? Apply a magnet and immediately every particle of iron will attach itself to it, while the brass remains behind. Thus if we see a company of true and false professors of religion, we may not be able to distinguish between them; but let Christ come among them, and all his sincere followers will be attracted towards him, as the steel is drawn to the magnet, while those who have none of his spirit, will remain at a distance.

Suppose we perceive a number of children playing together in the street, we could not, without previous knowledge, determine who are their parents, or where are their homes. But let one of them receive an injury, or get into any trouble, and we learn who are his parents, for he immediately runs to them for relief. Thus it is with the Christian and the man of the world. While we observe them together, pursuing the same employments, and placed in the same circumstances, we may not be able at once to distinguish them. But let afflictions come upon them and we are no longer at a loss; for the man of the world seeks relief in earthly comforts, while the Christian flies to his heavenly Father, his refuge and support in the day of trouble.

FEAR AND HOPE

True religion consists in a proper mixture of fear of God, and of hope in his mercy; and wherever either of these is entirely wanting, there can be no true religion. God has joined these things, and we ought by no means to put them asunder. He cannot take pleasure in those who fear him with a slavish fear, without hoping in his mercy, because they seem to consider him as a cruel and tyrannical being, who has no mercy or goodness in his nature; and, besides, they implicitly charge him with falsehood, by refusing to believe and hope in his invitations and offers of mercy. On the other hand, he cannot be pleased with those who pretend to hope in his mercy without fearing him; for they insult him by supposing that there is nothing in him which ought to be feared; and in addition to this, they make him a liar, by disbelieving his awful threatenings denounced against sinners, and call in question his authority, by refusing to obey him. Those only who both fear him and hope in his mercy, give him the honor that is due to his name.

THE LAW HONORED IN THE SINNER'S SALVATION

That the gospel method of justification by faith in Christ secures the honor of the law, will appear evident if we consider the views and feelings which it requires of all who would be justified and saved by this method. These views and feelings, taken collectively, are called repentance and faith. Repentance consists in hatred of sin, and sorrow on account of it. But sin is a transgression of the law. The penitent then hates and mourns for every transgression of the law of which he has been guilty. But no man can sincerely hate and mourn over his transgressions of any law, unless he sees and feels that it is a just and good law. If he does not see this, if the law which he has transgressed appears in his view unjust, or not good, he will hate and condemn, not himself, but the law and the lawmaker. Every real penitent then sees and acknowledges that the law which he has violated, is holy, and just, and good and glorious; that he is justly condemned by it, and that he should have no reason to complain of God, if he were left to perish forever. He can say, "I deserve the curse, and let no one ever think hardly of God, or of his law, though I should perish forever." And can those who exercise, or those who inculcate such feelings as these, be justly accused of making void, or of dishonoring the law? Do they not rather honor and establish it, by taking part with it against themselves, by saying, the law is right, and we only are wrong? To place this in a still clearer light, permit me to throw into the form of a dialogue, the feelings which a penitent, believing sinner exercises and expresses, when he applies to Christ to be justified or pardoned. Let us suppose the Savior to say to such a person, as he did to those who applied to him for relief, while on earth, "What wilt thou that I should do for thee?" "Save me, Lord, from my sins, and from the punishment which they deserve." "In what do thy sins consist?" "They consist, Lord, in numberless transgressions of God's law." "Is that law unjust?" "Lord, it is most just." "Why, then, didst thou transgress it?" "Because, O Lord, my heart was rebellious and perverse." "Canst thou offer no excuse, no pleas of extenuation of thy sins?" "None, Lord; I am altogether without excuse, nor do I wish to offer any." "Is not the punishment with which thou art threatened too severe?" "No, Lord, I deserve it all; nor can I escape it but through thy rich mercy and sovereign grace." Such is, in effect, the language of every one who applies to Christ for salvation; such the feelings implied in the exercise of repentance and faith.

The gospel method of justification sets before us new and powerful motives to obey the law. For instance, it presents God, the Lawgiver, in a new, and most interesting and affecting light. It shows him to us as the God and Father of our Lord Jesus Christ, displaying the most wonderful compassion for our lost and guilty race, and so loving our revolted world, as to give his only begotten Son to die for its offenses. Of all the attitudes in which God was ever revealed to his creatures, this is incomparably the most interesting and affecting. It is indeed interesting to view him as our Creator, our Sovereign, our Preserver and Benefactor; and we are sacredly bound to regard him, in these characters, with gratitude, reverence and love. But how much more interesting to see him pitying the sorrows which our sins against Him had brought upon us, and taking his only Son out of his bosom, to give him up as a ransom to redeem us from those sorrows! If God said to Abraham, "Now I know that thou lovest me, seeing thou hast not withheld thy son, thine only son, from me," (Gen. 22:12) well may we say to God, "Lord, now we know that thou lovest us, that thou dost not willingly punish us, that thou hast no pleasure in our death, since thou hast given thy Son, thine only and well-beloved Son, to die on the cross for our sins." Thus the gospel method of salvation by revealing God to us in this most interesting and affecting light, powerfully urges us to love him, to love his law, to repent of having disobeyed it, and to obey it hereafter.

Suppose human legislators could write their laws upon the hearts of their subjects. Would they not then secure obedience far more effectually than they can now do, by all the penalties which they annex to a violation of their laws? If they could give all their subjects a disposition to abhor murder, theft, injustice and fraud, would they not secure life and property in the most perfect manner? Just so, if the law of God can be written in men's hearts, if his love can be shed abroad in them, if they can be made holy, it will secure obedience to that law far more effectually than all the thunders and lightnings of Sinai.

ADAM OUR REPRESENTATIVE

It is sometimes asked, how it can be right that we should suffer in consequence of the sins of our first parents. In the first place, it is right because we imitate their example, and thus justify their conduct. We break the covenant, and disobey the law of God, as well as they. Another answer may be given by considering the subject in a different light. The angels who kept not their first estate, had no covenant head or representative, but each one stood for himself. Yet they fell. God was therefore pleased, when he made man, to adopt a different constitution of things; and since it had appeared that holy beings, endowed with every possible advantage for obeying God's law, would disobey it and ruin themselves, he thought proper, instead of leaving us, like the angels, to stand for ourselves, to appoint a covenant with him. Now, let us suppose for a moment, that we, and all the human race, had been brought into existence at once, and that God had proposed to us, that we should choose one of our number to be our representative, and to enter into covenant with him on our behalf. Should we not, with one voice, have chosen our first parent for this responsible office? Should we not have said, "He is a perfect man, and bears the image and likeness of God? If anyone must stand or fall for us, let him be the man." Now, since the angels, who stood for themselves, fell, why should we wish to stand for ourselves? And if we must have a representative to stand for us, why should we complain, when God has chosen the same person for this office, that we should have chosen, had we been in existence, and capable of choosing for ourselves?

CHRIST OUR REPRESENTATIVE

Christ "bore our sins" in the same sense in which the Jewish sacrifices, under the law, were said to bear the sins of him in whose behalf they were presented. The lamb which was offered did not itself become a sinner; and as little did Christ, our great Sacrifice, become sinful by bearing our sins. When, therefore, it is said that God laid on Him the iniquities of us all, and that He bore our sins in His own body on the tree, the meaning is, that God laid on Him, and that He bore the punishment which our sins deserved. Our sins were, by His own consent, imputed to Him, or as the word signifies, laid to His account: and He, in consequence, though innocent, was treated as a sinner.

DIVINE ATTRIBUTES FULLY SATISFIED

It is a maxim in divine, as well as in human laws, that what a man does by another, he does by himself. Now, in and by Christ, their surety, all who believe have done and suffered everything which the divine law, and consequently which justice, required. In him, they have obeyed the law perfectly, in him, they have suffered the curse which is due to sin. He was made sin for them, they are made righteous in him; and thus he is the end of the law for righteousness to every one that believes. The law of God is more highly honored by the obedience, and the justice of God more clearly displayed in the sufferings, of so exalted a personage, than they could have been by the obedience or the sufferings of the whole human race. Then, in the plan of redemption, God appears to be, at once, a just God and a Savior; thus he can be just and yet the justifier of him that believeth in Jesus; and justice and truth, as well as mercy and peace, (see Psalm 85:10,11) will welcome to heaven every redeemed sinner who is brought there through the merits of Christ. Thus we see that these divine attributes, which were set at variance by the fall of the first Adam, are reunited and satisfied by the atonement of the second. Mercy may now say, "I am satisfied, for my petitions in behalf of wretched man have been answered, and countless millions of that ruined race will sing the praises of boundless mercy forever and ever." Truth may say, "I am satisfied, for God's veracity and faithfulness remain inviolate, notwithstanding the salvation of sinners; and not one word that he has ever spoken, has failed of its full accomplishment." Justice may say, "I am satisfied, for the honor of the law over which I watch, has been secured; sin has met with deserved punishment; the Prince of life has died to satisfy my claims; and God has shown the whole universe that he loves me, even better than he loves his only Son; for when that Son cried, in agony, Father, spare me, and I demanded that he should not be spared, God listened to my demands rather than to his cries." Finally, Peace may say, "I am satisfied, for I have been permitted to proclaim peace on earth, and have seen God reconciling a rebellious world to himself. Come, then, my sister attributes, Mercy, Truth and Righteousness, let us once more be united in perfect harmony, and join to admire the plan which thus reconciles us to each other."

SINNERS PARDONED FOR CHRIST'S SAKE

It was highly proper that the unexampled benevolence, humility, and other graces which Christ displayed in condescending to obey, suffer and die, in our stead, should receive from his righteous Father a suitable reward; and that God should manifest, in a signal and illustrious manner, his approbation of such unequaled goodness, to all his intelligent creatures. But the Son of God neither needed, nor could receive any reward for himself; for he is the brightness of the Father's glory, and the express image of his person, and possesses in the highest degree, all possible perfection, glory, and felicity. Since, therefore, it was necessary that Christ should be rewarded, and since he needed no reward for himself, his Father was pleased, in the covenant of redemption, to promise him what would be to his benevolent heart the greatest of all rewards. He promised him that if he would make his soul an offering for sin, he should have a seed and people to serve him; and that all his spiritual seed, all his chosen people, who were given him by his Father, should, for his sake, and as a reward of his obedience, suffering and death, be saved from the guilt and power of sin, be adopted as the children of

God, made joint heirs with Christ of the heavenly inheritance, and receive, through him, everything necessary to prepare and qualify them for its enjoyment. Thus God bestows everlasting life, glory and felicity on guilty rebels, and merely for the sake of Christ, and with a view to convince all intelligent beings, that he is infinitely well pleased with the holy benevolence which his Son displayed, when he consented to die in their stead.

GOD'S PERFECTIONS DISPLAYED IN THE PLAN OF REDEMPTION

There is more of God, more of his essential glory displayed in bringing one sinner to repentance, and forgiving his sins, than in all the wonders of creation. In this work, creatures may see, if I may so express it, the very heart of God. From this work, angels themselves have probably learned more of God's moral character than they have ever been able to learn before. They knew before that God was wise and powerful; for they had seen him create a world. They knew that he was good; for he had made them perfectly holy and happy. They knew that he was just; for they had seen him cast down their own rebellious brethren from heaven to hell for their sins. But until they saw him give repentance and remission of sins through Christ, they did not know that he was merciful; they did not know that he could pardon a sinner. And O! what an hour was that in heaven when this great truth was first made known; when the first penitent was pardoned! Then a new song was put into the mouths of angels; and while, with unutterable emotions of wonder, love, and praise, they began to sing it, their voices swelled to a higher pitch, and they experienced joys unfelt before. O how did the joyful sounds, "his mercy endureth forever," spread from choir to choir, echo through the high arches of heaven, and thrill through every enraptured angelic breast; and how did they cry, with one voice, "Glory to God in the highest, on earth peace, and good will to man!"

On no page less ample than that of the eternal, all enfolding mind which devised the gospel plan of salvation, can its glories be displayed; nor by any inferior mind can they be fully comprehended. Suffice it to say, that here the moral character of Jehovah shines full-orbed and complete; here all the fulness of the Godhead, all the insufferable splendors of Deity burst, at once, upon our aching sight. Here the manifold perfections of God, holiness and goodness, justice and mercy, truth and grace, majesty and condescension, hatred of sin and compassion for sinners, are harmoniously blended, like the party-colored rays of solar light, in one pure blaze of dazzling whiteness; here, rather than on any other of his works, he founds his claims to the highest admiration, gratitude, and love of his creatures; here is the work which ever has called forth, and which through eternity will continue to call forth, the most rapturous praises of the celestial choirs, and feed the ever-glowing fires of devotion in their breasts; for the glory which shines in the gospel, is the glory which illuminates heaven, and the Lamb that was slain is the light thereof.

CONDITION OF THE WORLD WITHOUT A SAVIOR

Would you learn the full extent of that wretchedness which sin tends to produce, you must follow it into the eternal world and descend into those regions where peace, where hope never comes; and there, by the light of revelation, behold sin tyrannizing over its wretched victims with uncontrollable fury; fanning the inextinguishable fire, and sharpening the tooth of the immortal worm. See angels and archangels, thrones and dominions, principalities and powers, stripped of all their primeval glory and beauty, bound in eternal chains, and burning with rage and malice against that Being, in whose presence they once rejoiced, and whose praises they once sung. See multitudes of the human race, in unutterable agonies of anguish and despair, cursing the gift, the Giver and Prolonger of their existence, and vainly wishing for annihilation, to put a period to their miseries. Follow them through the long, long ages of eternity, and see them sinking deeper and deeper in the bottomless abyss of ruin, perpetually blaspheming God because of their plagues, and receiving the punishment of these blasphemies in continued additions to their wretchedness. Such are the wages of sin; such the doom of the finally impenitent. From these depths of anguish and despair, look up to the mansions of the blessed, and see to what a height of glory and felicity the grace of God will raise every sinner that repenteth. See those who are thus favored in unutterable ecstasies of joy, love and praise, contemplating God, face to face, reflecting his perfect image, shining with a splendor like that of their glorious Redeemer, filled with all the fulness of Deity, and bathing in those rivers of pleasure which flow forever at God's right hand. Follow them in their endless flight towards perfection. See them rapidly mounting from height to height, darting onward with increasing swiftness, and unwearied wing, towards that infinity which they will never reach. View this, and then say whether infinite holiness and benevolence may not, with propriety, rejoice over every sinner that repenteth.

Do any doubt whether the gospel is indeed glad tidings of great joy? Come with me to the garden of Eden. Look back to the hour which succeeded man's apostasy. See the golden chain which bound man to God, and God to man, sundered, apparently forever, and this wretched world, groaning under the weight of human guilt, and its Maker's curse, sinking down, far down, into a bottomless abyss of misery and despair. See that tremendous Being who is a consuming fire, encircling it on every side, and wrapping it, as it were, in an atmosphere of flame. Hear from his lips the tremendous sentence, Man has sinned, and man must die. See the king of terrors advancing with gigantic strides to execute the awful sentence, the grave expanding her marble jaw as to receive whatever might fall before his wide-wasting scythe, and hell beneath, yawning dreadful, to engulf forever its guilty, helpless, despairing victims. Such was the situation of our ruined race after the apostasy. Endeavor, if you can, to realize its horrors. Endeavor, to forget, for a moment, that you ever heard of Christ or his gospel. View yourselves as immortal beings hastening to eternity, with the curse of Gods' broken law, like a flaming sword, pursuing you; death, with his dart dipped in mortal poison, awaiting you; a dark cloud, fraught with the lightnings of divine vengeance, rolling over your heads; your feet standing in slippery places, in darkness, and the bottomless pit beneath expecting your fall. Then, when not only all hope, but all possibility of escape, seemed taken away, suppose the flaming sword suddenly quenched; the sting extracted; the sun of righteousness bursting forth and painting a rainbow on the before threatening cloud; a golden ladder let down from the opening gates of heaven, while a choir of angels, swiftly descending, exclaim, Behold, we bring you glad tidings of great joy, for unto you is born a Savior, who is Christ the Lord. Would you, could you, while contemplating such a scene, and listening to the angelic message, doubt whether it communicated glad tidings? Would you not rather unite with them in exclaiming, "Glad tidings! Glad tidings! Glory to God in the highest, that there is peace on earth, and good will to men" ?

CHRIST OUR EXAMPLE

It was highly important and desirable that our great High Priest should not only obtain for us the heavenly inheritance but also go before us, in the path which leads to it; that he should not only describe Christianity in his discourses, but exemplify it in his life and conversation. This our blessed Savior has done. In him we see pure and undefiled religion embodied. In him Christianity lives and breathes. And how amiable, how interesting does she there appear! How convincing, how animating is our Savior's example! How loudly, how persuasively does his conduct preach! Would you learn submission to parental authority? See him, notwithstanding his exalted character, cheerfully subjecting himself to the will of his parents, and laboring with them, as a carpenter, for almost thirty years. Would you learn contentment with a poor and low condition? See him destitute of a place where to lay his head. Would you learn active beneficence? See him going about doing good. Would you learn to be fervent and constant in devotional exercises? See him rising for prayer before the dawn of day. Would you learn in what manner to treat you brethren? See him washing his disciples' feet. Would you learn filial piety? See him forgetting his sufferings, while in the agonies of death, to provide another son for his desolate mother. Would you learn in what manner to pray for relief under afflictions? See him in the garden. Would you learn how to bear insults and injuries? See him on the cross. In short, there is no Christian grace or virtue, proper for a perfectly innocent being to possess, which is not beautifully exemplified in his life; and there is scarce any situation, however perplexing, in which the Christian, who is at a loss to know how he ought to act, may not derive sufficient instruction from the example of his divine Master.

CHRIST A TEACHER

A celebrated philosopher of antiquity, who was accustomed to receive large sums from his pupils, in return for his instructions, was one day accosted by an indigent youth, who requested admission into the number of his disciples. "And what," said the sage, "will you give me in return?" "I will give you myself," was the reply. "I accept the gift," answered the sage, "and engage to restore you to yourself, at some future period, much more valuable than you are at present." In similar language does our great Teacher address those who apply to him for instruction, conscious that they are unable to purchase his instructions, and offering to give him themselves. He will readily accept the gift; he will educate them for heaven, and will, at length, restore them to themselves, incomparably more wise, more happy, and more valuable, than when he received them.

CHRIST, THE BELOVED FRIEND

Does not our Friend as far excel all other friends, as heaven exceeds earth, as eternity exceeds time, as the Creator surpasses his creatures? If you doubt this, bring together all the glory, pomp and beauty of the world; nay, assemble everything that is great and excellent in all the worlds that ever were created; collect all the creatures which the breath of Omnipotence ever summoned into being; and we, on our parts, will place beside them our Savior and Friend, that you may see whether they will bear a comparison with him. Look, then, first at your idols; behold the vast assemblage which you have collected, and then turn and contemplate our Beloved. See all the fulness of the Godhead, dwelling in one who is meek and lowly as a child. See his countenance beaming with ineffable glories, full of mingled majesty, condescension and love, and hear the soul-reviving invitations which proceed from his lips. See that hand in which dwells everlasting strength, swaying the scepter of universal empire over all creatures and all worlds; see his arms expanded to receive and embrace returning sinners, while his heart, a bottomless, shoreless ocean of benevolence, overflows with tenderness, compassion, and love. In a word, see in him all natural and moral excellence, personified, and embodied in a resplendent form, compared with whose effulgent, dazzling glories, the splendors of the meridian sun are dark. He speaks, and a world emerges from nothing. He frowns, and it sinks to nothing again. He waves his hand, and all the creatures which you have collected to rival him, sink and disappear. Such, O sinner, is our Beloved, and such is our Friend. Will you not then embrace him as your Friend? If you can be persuaded to do this, you will find that the one half, nay, that the thousandth part has not been told you.

All the excellency, glory and beauty, which is found in men or angels, flows from Christ, as a drop of water from the ocean, or a ray of light from the sun. If, then, you supremely love the creature, can you wonder that Christians should love the Creator? If you admire an image in a glass, is it strange that they should admire the sun by which it was painted? Can you wonder that those who behold the glory of God, in the face of Jesus Christ, should be sweetly drawn to him by the cords of love, and lose their fondness for created glories? All that you love and admire, and wish for, in creatures, and indeed infinitely more, they find in him. Do you wish for a friend possessed of power to protect you? Our Friend possesses all power in heaven and earth, and is able to save even to the uttermost. Do you wish for a wise and experienced friend? In Christ are hid all the treasures of wisdom and knowledge. Do you wish for a tender, compassionate friend? Christ is tenderness and compassion itself. Do you wish for a faithful, unchangeable friend? With Christ there is no variableness, nor shadow of turning; but he is the same yesterday, today, and forever. His unchangeable love will ever prompt him to make his people happy; his unerring wisdom will point out the best means to promote their happiness; and his infinite power will enable him to employ those means. In all these respects, our Beloved is more than another beloved; for creatures are not always disposed to render us happy: when they are disposed to do it, they do not always know how; and when they know how, they are often unable. Better is it, therefore, to trust in Christ, than to put confidence in princes.

CHRIST'S INVITATIONS
TO THE WEARY AND OPPRESSED

To all who are afflicted either in body, mind or estate; all whose worldly hopes and prospects have been blasted by losses and disappointments; all who are weeping over the grave of some near and dear relative; the language of Christ is, "Cast your burden upon me, and I will sustain thee; call upon me now in the day of trouble, and I will answer thee. You have found that earthly friends and relations die; come, then, to me, and find a Friend who cannot die; one who will never leave nor forsake you, in life or death. You have found that treasures laid up on earth, make to themselves wings and fly away; come, then, to me, and I will give you treasures which never fail, and make you heirs of the heavenly inheritance. No longer spend your money for that which is not bread, and your labor for that which satisfieth not; but hearken diligently to my call, and come unto me; hear, and your souls shall live; and I will make an everlasting covenant with you, even the sure mercies of David."

CHRIST'S DISPLEASURE AT SIN

We read of Christ's being angry but three times during the whole period of his residence on earth, and in each of those instances, his anger was excited not by insults or injuries offered to himself, but by conduct which tended to interrupt or frustrate his benevolent exertions in doing good. When he was reviled as a man gluttonous, intemperate, and possessed by a devil, he was not angry; when he was buffeted, spit upon, and crowned with thorns, he was not angry; when nailed to the cross, and loaded with insults in his last agonies, he was not angry. But when his disciples forbade parents to bring their infant children to receive his blessing; when Peter endeavored to dissuade him from dying for sinners; and when sinners, by their hardness of heart, rendered his intended death of no service to themselves; then he was angry and much displeased.

Suppose a person whom you had found deserted in the streets when an infant, and adopted and educated as your own, should, when arrived to manhood, rob and attempt to murder you. Suppose him tried, convicted, condemned, and confined to await the execution of his sentence. You pity him, forgive him, and wish to save his life. You fly to the proper authority, and after much expense and labor, obtain an assurance that if he will confess his crime, he shall be pardoned. You hasten to his dungeon to communicate the happy intelligence. But he refuses to hear you, believe you, or confess his fault; regards you with aversion, suspicion or contempt, and turns a deaf ear to your prayers and entreaties. Would you not be unutterably shocked, disappointed and grieved? What, then, must be the feelings of Christ, when treated in a similar manner by those whom he died to save! Well may he look on them with anger, being grieved for the hardness of their hearts.

Come with us a moment to Calvary. See the meek sufferer standing, with hands fast bound, in the midst of his enemies, sinking under the weight of his cross, and lacerated in every part, by the thorny reeds with which he had been scourged. See the savage, ferocious soldiers raising, with rude violence, his sacred body, forcing it down upon the cross, wresting and extending his limbs, and, with remorseless cruelty, forcing through his hands and feet the ragged spikes which were to fix him on it. See the Jewish priests and rulers watching, with looks of malicious pleasure, the horrid scene, and attempting to increase his sufferings by scoffs and blasphemies. Now contemplate attentively the countenance of the wonderful sufferer, which seems like heaven opening in the midst of hell, and tell me what it expresses. You see it indeed full of anguish, but it expresses nothing like impatience, resentment or revenge. On the contrary, it beams with pity, benevolence, and forgiveness. It perfectly corresponds with the prayer, which, raising his mild, imploring eyes to heaven, he pours forth to God; "Father, forgive them, for they know not what they do." Christian, look at your Master, and learn how to suffer. Sinner, look at your Savior, and learn to admire, to imitate, and to forgive.

THE SUFFERINGS OF CHRIST

It has been supposed by many, that the sufferings of Christ were rather apparent than real; or at least that his abundant consolations, and his knowledge of the happy consequences which would result from his death, rendered his sorrows comparatively light, and almost converted them to joys. But never was supposition more erroneous. Jesus Christ was as truly a man as either of us; and, as man, he was as really susceptible of grief, as keenly alive to pain and reproach, and as much averse from pain and suffering, as any of the descendants of Adam. As to divine consolation and supports, they were at all times bestowed on him in a very sparing manner, and in the season of his greatest extremity entirely withheld; and though a knowledge of the happy consequences which would result from his sufferings rendered him willing to endure them, it did not in the smallest degree take off their edge, or render him insensible to pain. No, his sufferings, instead of being less, were incomparably greater than they appeared to be. No finite mind can conceive of their extent, nor was any of the human race ever so well entitled to the appellation of the man of sorrows, as the man Jesus Christ.

LOVE OF CHRIST

In order to form some faint conception of the love of Christ, suppose, my Christian friends, that all your toils and sufferings were ended, and you were safely arrived in heaven, the rest which remains for the people of God.

Suppose that you were there crowned with glory, and honor, and immortality, listening with unutterable ecstasies to the song of the redeemed, contemplating the ineffable, unveiled glories of Jehovah, drinking full draughts from those rivers of pleasure which flow forever at his right hand, and tasting those joys which the heart of man hath not conceived. What would tempt you to revisit this vale of tears, commence anew the wearisome journey of life, and encounter all the toils, the temptations, the sufferings and sorrows which attend it? Must it not be love stronger than death, love such as you cannot conceive of, which would induce you to do this? How infinite, how inconceivable, then, must have been the love which brought down the Son of God from the celestial world to redeem our ruined race! which led him to exchange the bosom of his Father for a veil of flesh; the adoration of angels for the scoffs and insults of sinners; and the enjoyment of eternal life for an accursed, painful and ignominious death! Nothing but love could have done this. Not all the powers of heaven, earth and hell combined, could have dragged him from his celestial throne, and wrested the scepter of the universe from his hands. No, it was love alone, divine, omnipotent love, which drew him down; it was in the bands of love that he was led a willing captive, through all the toils and sufferings of a laborious life; and it was these bands which bound him at the bar of Pilate, which fettered his arm of everlasting strength, and prevented his blasting his murderers.

Unless we could ascend into heaven, and see the glory and happiness which our Redeemer left; unless we could descend into the grave, and learn the depths of wretchedness to which he sank; unless we would weigh, as in a balance, all the trials, toils and sufferings of his life;

never, never can we know the immeasurable extent of his love. But these things we cannot do. None but the omniscient God knows what he felt, or what he suffered; none but the omniscient God, therefore, knows the extent of his love. To think of the love of Christ, is like trying to conceive of existence which has no beginning, and of power which can make something of nothing. Tongue cannot describe it; finite minds cannot conceive of it; angels faint under it; and those who know most of it can only say, with inspiration, that it passeth knowledge.

SELF-DENIAL OF CHRIST

The life of Christ was one of self-denial. He denied himself, for thirty years, all the glories and felicity of the heavenly world; and exposed himself to all the pains and sorrows of a life on earth. He denied himself the praises and adorations of saints and angels; and exposed himself to the blasphemies and reproaches of men. He denied himself the presence and enjoyment of God; and exposed himself to the society of publicans and sinners. He denied himself everything that nature desires; He exposed himself to everything she dreads and abhors; to poverty, contempt, pain and death. When he entered on his glorious and godlike design, He renounced all regard to his own comfort and convenience, and took up the cross, a cross infinitely heavier and more painful than any of his disciples had been called to bear, and continued to carry it through a rough and thorny road, till his human nature, exhausted, sunk under the weight. In short, he consi- dered himself, his time, his talents, his reputation, his happiness, his very existence, as not his own, but another's; and he ever employed them accordingly. He lived not for himself, he died not for himself; but for others he lived, and for others he died.

HE SHALL SEE OF THE TRAVAIL OF HIS SOUL

How great, how inconceivable will be our Savior's happiness, after the final consummation of all things! Then the plan for which our world was formed will be completed. Then every member of the church, for the sake of which he loved and visited our world, will have been brought home to heaven, to be with him where he is. And if he loved, and rejoiced, and delighted in them before they existed, and before they knew and loved him, how will he love and rejoice in them when he sees them surrounding his throne, perfectly resembling himself in body and soul; loving him with unutterable love, contemplating him with ineffable delight, and praising him as their Deliverer from sin, and death, and hell; as the author of all their everlasting glory and felicity! Then, O blessed, animating thought! he will be amply rewarded for all his sufferings, and for all his love to our ruined race; then his people shall cease to grieve and offend him; then they shall no longer degrade him by weak, confused, inadequate conceptions of his person, character, and work; for then shall they see as they are seen, and know even as they are known. Then the whole church shall be presented to him, a glorious church, without spot or blemish, or imperfection; and shall be as a crown of glory in the hand of the Lord, and as a royal diadem in the hand of our God. Then, O Zion, as a bridegroom rejoiceth over the bride, so shall thy God rejoice over thee. Then shall thy sun no more go down, nor thy moon withdraw itself; but the Lord shall be thine everlasting light, and thy God, thy glory; and the days of thy mourning, and of thy Savior's suffering, shall be ended.

If we love, and prize, and rejoice in any object, in proportion to the labor, pain, and expense which it has cost us to obtain it, how greatly must Christ love, and prize, and rejoice in every penitent sinner! His love and joy must be unutterable, inconceivable, infinite. For once, I rejoice that our Savior's toils and sufferings were so great, since the greater they were, the greater must be his love for us, and his joy in our conversion. And if he thus rejoiceth over one sinner that repenteth, what must be his joy, when all his people are collected, out of every tongue, and kindred, and people, and nation, and presented spotless before his Father's throne! What a full tide of felicity will pour in upon him, and how will his benevolent heart expand with unutterable delight, when, contemplating the countless myriads of the redeemed, he says, "Were it not for my sufferings, all these immortal beings would have been, throughout eternity, as miserable, and now they will be as happy, as God can make them! It is enough. I see of the travail of my soul, and am satisfied."

CONDESCENSION AND LOVE OF CHRIST

The meanest beggar, the vilest wretch, the most loathsome, depraved, abandoned sinner, is perfectly welcome to the arms and the heart of the Savior, if he comes with the temper of the penitent prodigal. To all who come with this temper, he ever lends a gracious ear; he listens to catch the first penitential sigh; he watches their first feeble step towards the path of duty; he prevents them with his grace, hastens to meet them, and while they are ready to sink at his feet with mingled shame, confusion and grief, he puts underneath them his everlasting arms, embraces, cheers, supports and comforts them; wipes away their tears, washes away their stains, clothes them with his righteousness, unites them to himself forever, and feeds them with the bread and water of life. Thus he binds up the broken reed, enkindles the smoking flax, and, like a most tender, compassionate shepherd, gathers the helpless lambs in his arms, and carries them in his bosom. Thus, by the condescending grace of our Immanuel, heaven is brought down to earth; the awful majesty, and inaccessible glories of Jehovah, are shrouded in a veil of flesh; a new and living way is opened for our return to God; and sinful, guilty worms of the dust may talk with their Maker face to face, as a man talketh with his friend.

Trembling sinner, despondent Christian, permit me to take you by the hand and lead you to Jesus. Why do you linger, why do you hang back? It is to Christ, it is to Jesus, it is to the Babe of Bethlehem, to a man like yourselves, to the meek and lowly Savior of sinners, that I would bring you. Here are no terrors, no flaming sword, no burning throne to appall you. Come, then, to his feet, to his arms, to his heart, which overflows with compassion for your perishing souls. Come and contemplate the glory of the only- begotten of the Father, full of grace and truth, and receive of his fulness grace for grace (John 1:14,16).

COMPASSION AND CONDESCENSION OF CHRIST

Fear not, says the Savior to his penitent, heartbroken disciple. Fear not, trembling, desponding soul. My glory, my perfections need not alarm thee, for they are all engaged on thy side, all pledged to secure thy salvation. Tell me not of thy sins. I will take them away. Tell me not of thy weakness, thy folly and ignorance. I have treasures of wisdom and knowledge, and strength for thee. Tell me not of the weakness of thy graces. My grace is sufficient for thee, for its riches are unsearchable. Tell me not of the difficulties which oppose thy salvation. Is any thing too hard for me? Tell me not that the favors thou art receiving are too great for thee. I know they are too great for thee to merit, but they are not too great for me to give. Nay, more, I will give thee greater things than these. I will not only continue to pardon thy sins, bear with thine infirmities, and heal thy backslidings; but give thee larger and larger measures of my grace, make thee more and more useful in the world, render thee more than a conqueror over all thine enemies, and at death wipe away forever all thy tears; receive thee to the mansions which my Father has prepared for thee in heaven, and cause thee to sit down with me on my throne forever and ever. Thus does Christ comfort those that mourn; thus he encourages the desponding, thus exalts those that humble themselves at his feet; and constrains them to cry, in admiring transports of gratitude and love, "Who, O who is a God like unto thee, forgiving iniquity, transgression and sin?"

Christ said to Mary, "Fear not; I know that you seek Jesus." If ye really seek Jesus, he says the same to you. Fear not; death, sorrow, sickness, anything. If they are blessed who seek Jesus, what must those be who have found him?

THE LANGUAGE OF PENITENCE

As our views of our own sinfulness, and of the abominable malignity of sin, are always in direct proportion to our views of the divine purity and glory, the Christian never appears to himself so unspeakably vile, so totally unworthy of his Savior's love, or so unfit to enjoy his presence, as at the very time when he is favored with these blessings, in the highest degree. The consequence is that he is astonished, confounded, crushed and overwhelmed by a display of goodness so undeserved, so unexpected. When he has perhaps been ready to conclude that he was a vile hypocrite, and to give up all for lost; or, if not to fear that God would bring upon him some terrible judgment for his sins, and make him an example to others; then to see his much-insulted Savior, his neglected Benefactor, his injured Friend, suddenly appear to deliver him from the consequences of his own folly and ingratitude; to see him come with smiles and blessings, when he expected nothing but upbraidings, threatenings, and scourges; it is too much; he knows not how to bear it; he scarcely dares take the consolation offered him; he thinks it must be all a delusion. Even when convinced beyond a doubt, that it is not so; when he feels the healing virtue of his kind Physician, pervading his whole soul, and sees him stooping to cleanse, to comfort, and embrace him, he shrinks back, involuntarily, as if the spotless Savior would be contaminated by his touch; sinks down ashamed and brokenhearted at his feet; feels unworthy and unable to look up; and the more condescendingly Christ stoops to embrace him, so much lower and lower does he sink in the dust. At length his emotions find utterance, and he cries, "O Lord, treat me not thus kindly. Such favors belong to those, only, who do not requite thy love as I have done. How can it be just, how can it be right to give them to one so undeserving? Thy kindness is lavished upon me in vain; thy mercies are thrown away upon one so incorrigibly vile. If thou pardon me now, I shall offend thee again; if thou heal my backslidings, I shall again wander from thee; if thou cleanse me, I shall again become polluted: thou must, O Lord, give me up; thou must leave me to perish, and bestow thy favors on those who are less unworthy, less incurably prone to offend thee." Such are often the feelings of the brokenhearted penitent; thus does he shrink from the mercy which pursues him, thus seems to plead against himself; and, though he desires and prizes nothing so much as his Savior's presence, feels constrained by a sense of his vileness and pollution, to ask him, and almost wish him to depart, and leave him to the fate which he so richly deserves.

JOY OF COMMUNING WITH GOD

At times, God is pleased to admit his children to nearer approaches, and more intimate degrees of fellowship with himself and his Son, Jesus Christ. He sends down the spirit of adoption into their hearts, whereby they are enabled to cry, "Abba, Father!" and to feel those lively affections of love, joy, trust, hope, reverence and dependence, which it is at once their duty and their happiness to exercise towards their Father in heaven. By the influences of the same Spirit he shines into their minds, to give them the light of the knowledge of the glory of God, in the face of Jesus Christ; causes his glory to pass before them, and makes them, in some measure, to understand the perfections of his nature. He also reveals to them the unutterable, inconceivable, unheard of things, which he has prepared for those who love him; applies to them his exceeding great and precious promises; makes them to know that great love wherewith he has loved them, and thus causes them to rejoice with joy unspeakable and full of glory. He shines in upon their souls with the dazzling, melting, overpowering beams of grace and mercy proceeding from the Sun of righteousness, gives them to know the heights and the depths, the lengths and the breadths, of the love of Christ, which passeth knowledge, and fills them with all the fulness of God. The Christian, in these bright, enraptured moments, while thus basking in beams of celestial light and splendor, forgets himself, forgets his existence, and is wholly absorbed in the ravishing, the ecstatic contemplation of uncreated beauty and loveliness. He endeavors to plunge himself into the boundless ocean of divine glory which opens to his views, and longs to be wholly swallowed up and lost in God. His whole soul goes forth in one intense flame of gratitude, admiration, love and desire. He contemplates, he wonders, he admires, he loves and adores. His soul dilates itself beyond its ordinary capacity, and expands to receive the flood of happiness which overwhelms it. All its desires are satisfied. It no longer inquires, "who will show us any good", but returns unto its rest, because the Lord hath dealt bountifully with it. The scanty, noisy, thirst-producing streams of worldly delight only increase the feverish desires of the soul; but the tide of joy which flows in upon the Christian, is silent, deep, full and satisfying. All the powers and faculties of his mind are lost, absorbed, and swallowed up on the contemplation of infinite glory. With an energy and activity unknown before, he roams and ranges through the ocean of light and love, where he can neither find a bottom nor a shore. No language can utter his feelings; but, with an emphasis, a meaning, an expression, which God alone could excite, and which he alone can understand, he breathes out the ardent emotions of his soul, in broken words, while he exclaims, "my Father and my God."

A CALL TO CHRISTIANS IN TIME OF A REVIVAL

Yes, O Christian, whoever you are, however tempted and distressed, however languishing and despairing you may be, the Master is come, and calleth for thee. He does, as it were, call thee by name, for he knows the names of his sheep; they are engraven on the palms of his hands, and he cannot forget them. His language is, "Where is this, and that, and the other one, among my flock, who used to watch for the tokens of my approach, and come at the sound of my voice? Why do they not come to welcome my return, and rejoice in my presence? Have they backslidden and wandered from my fold? Go, and tell them that their Shepherd is come, and calleth for them. Say unto them, 'How long will ye go about, O backsliding people? Return unto me, and I will heal your backslidings.' Are they tempted and distressed? Go, and tell them that their High Priest and Intercessor, one who has been in all points tempted like as they are, and who can therefore be touched with the feeling of their infirmities, is come, and calleth for them to spread their temptations and afflictions before him. Are they borne down with a load of guilt, and the weight of their sins against me, so that they are ashamed to look me in the face? Tell them that I will receive them graciously, and love them freely. Are they carried away by their spiritual enemies, and bound in the fetters of vice, so that they cannot come to welcome me? Tell them that I am come to proclaim deliverance to the captives, and the opening of the prison to them that are bound; to rescue the lambs of my flock from the paw of the lion and the jaws of the bear. Are they oppressed with fears that they shall one day perish by the hand of their enemies? Go and tell them that my sheep never perish, and that none shall finally pluck them out of my hand. Are they slumbering and sleeping, insensible of my approach? Go and awake them with the cry, "Behold the bridegroom cometh; go ye out to meet him."

It is profitable for the children of God often to reflect on what they formerly were, to mediate on their once wretched and helpless condition, to look to the rock whence they were hewn, and to the pit whence they were digged. Look back, then, Christians, to the time when you, who are now the children of God, the members of Christ, and the temples of the Holy Spirit, were the enemies of God, the despisers of his Son, and the willing slaves of the father of lies, who wrought in you as children of disobedience; when your hearts were hard as the nether millstone, your understandings darkened and alienated from the life of God; your wills stubborn, perverse and rebellious; your affections madly bent on the pleasures of sin; and every imagination of the thoughts of your hearts was evil only, and continually evil. Look back with shame and self-abhorrence to the time when you lived without God in the world, when you drank in iniquity like water, serving diverse lusts and vanities, and fulfilling the desires of the flesh and the mind; casting God's law behind your backs, stifling the remonstrances of conscience quenching the influences of the divine Spirit, neglecting the Holy Scriptures, and coming to the house of God, from Sabbath to Sabbath, not to honor him in the assembly of his saints, or to learn your duty; but to mock him with pretended worship, while your hearts were far from him. How many calls and invitations did you there slight! How many sermons did you hear as though you heard not! How many prayers were offered up in your presence, while you, perhaps, never considered, for a moment, in what you were engaged, but suffered your thoughts to wander to the ends of the earth! Even then, God was watching over you for good; and yet how ungratefully did you requite him! How many mercies did you receive without making one grateful acknowledgment! How did you strive to provoke him to jealousy, and lead him, if possible, to alter his gracious designs in your favor! A rebel against God, a crucifier of

Christ, a resister of the divine Spirit, a slave of Satan, a child of wrath, an heir of hell; such, O Christian, was once thy character; and nothing, in human view, was then before thee, but a fearful looking for of judgment and fiery indignation.

When we remember an absent friend, we usually think with deep interest of the place where he is, of the business in which he is engaged, and of the time when we shall meet him. Christians, you know where your Master is. You know what he is doing. You know that he now appears in the presence of God for you; that he ever liveth to make intercession for you; and that, ere long, you shall see him and be with him. Think then, much and often, of the heaven where he resides, of the perfect wisdom, fidelity, and constancy, with which he there manages your concerns. Remember that he watches for you while you sleep; that he labors for you while you are idle; that he intercedes for you, even while you are sinning against him. Will you, then, ever sin? Will you, while awake, ever be idle? Will you be unfaithful, or slothful in laboring for him, while he is ever active and faithful in promoting your interests?

CHRISTIANS, MEMBERS OF THE BODY OF CHRIST

Since Christ is the head of the body of which Christians are members, he has a right to expect the same services from them, which we expect from our members. Now what we expect from our members is, that every one, in its proper place, should perform the services allotted it; executing the purposes, and obeying the commands of the head. We do not expect that each member should have a separate will, or pursue a separate interest, or act in any respect as if it were independent. If any part of our bodies does not fulfill these expectations, and yield prompt and implicit obedience to our will, we conclude it to be diseased; and if the acts of the will produce no effect upon it, we conclude it to be dead, and remove it, if possible, as a useless encumbrance. We further expect that our members, instead of attempting to provide, each one, for its own wants, will depend upon the wisdom and foresight of the head, for all necessary supplies. In a word, we know that it is the part of the head to plan, direct and provide, and the part of the members to obey and execute. Precisely similar are the duties of Christians, considered as the members of Christ. No Christian must have a separate will, or a separate interest of his own, or act, in any respect, as if he were an insulated, independent individual. As there is but one head, so there must be but one governing, guiding will, and that must be the will of Christ. If any neglect to execute his will, they are spiritually diseased; and if this neglect be habitual, they are spiritually dead, and were never really united to Christ, for his real members never die. It is also their duty to depend on him for every thing, for the supply of all their temporal and spiritual necessities; and never to attempt any thing but in reliance on his wisdom, grace and strength. As well may our feet walk safely, or our hands work skillfully, without assistance and guidance from the head, as Christians can perform any service without the grace of Christ their head, in whom are laid up all the treasures of wisdom, and knowledge, and grace.

THE CHRISTIAN'S CONSOLATION

Christians, a man now fills the throne of heaven. And who is this man? Believer, mark it well. It is a man who is not ashamed to call you brother. It is a man who can be touched with the feeling of your infirmities, for he has been in all points tempted like as you are, yet without sin. Whatever your sorrows or trials may be, he knows by experience how to sympathize with you. Has your Heavenly Father forsaken you, so that you walk in darkness and see no light? He well remembers what he felt, when he cried, "My God, my God, why hast thou forsaken me?" Has Satan wounded you with his fiery darts? He remembers how sorely his own heart was bruised when he wrestled with principalities and powers, and crushed the head of the prince of darkness. Are you assaulted with various and distressing temptations? Christ was tempted to doubt whether he were the Son of God, to presume upon his Father's love, and to worship the father of lies. Are you pressed down with a complication of sorrows, so as to despair even of life? The soul of Christ was once exceeding sorrowful, even unto death. Are you mourning for the danger of unbelieving friends? Christ's own brethren did not believe in him. Does the world persecute and despise you, or are your enemies those of your own household? Christ was despised and rejected of men, and his own relations stigmatized him as a madman. Are you suffering under slanderous and unjust accusations? Christ was called a man gluttonous, and a wine-bibber, a friend of publicans and sinners. Are you struggling with the evils of poverty? Jesus had not where to lay his head. Do Christian friends forsake, or treat you unkindly? Christ was denied and forsaken by his own disciples. Are you distressed with fears of death? Christ has entered the dark valley that he might destroy death. O, then, banish all your fears. Look at your merciful High Priest who is passed unto the heavens, and triumphantly exclaim with the apostle, "Who shall separate us from the love of Christ?"

The professed disciple of Christ, who desponds and trembles, when he hears his Master calling him to go on to perfection, may derive courage and support from looking at the promises of Christ, and at their Author. Among the blessings promised, you will find everything which any man can need, to assist him in arriving at perfection. There are promises of light and direction to find the path which leads to it; promises of assistance to walk in that path; promises of strength to resist and overcome all opposition; promises of remedies to heal us when wounded, of cordials to invigorate us when faint, and of most glorious rewards to crown the end of our course. You will hear Jehovah saying, "Fear not, for I am with thee; be not dismayed, for I am thy God: I will strengthen thee; yea, I will help thee; yea, I will uphold thee with the right hand of my righteousness. Though thou art in thyself but a worm, thou shalt thresh the mountains, and beat them small as the dust." Look next at him who gives these promises. It is one who is almighty, and who therefore can fulfill them. It is one who cannot lie, and therefore will fulfill them. It is one who possesses all power in heaven and on earth; one whose treasures of grace are unsearchable and inexhaustible; one in whom dwells all the fulness of the Godhead bodily. With all this fulness, faith indissolubly unites us. Say, then, ye who despond and tremble, when you contemplate the almost immeasurable distance between your own moral characters and that of Christ, what, except faith in these promises and in their Author, is necessary, to support, encourage, and animate you in going on to perfection? If Christ himself is perfect; if faith makes you members of this perfect head; if it causes his fulness to flow into your souls, then it is most evident that he can and will enable all, who exercise faith in him, to imitate his example, and finally to become perfect as he is perfect.

Let not the Christian listen to the suggestions of indolence, despondency and unbelief; but let him listen rather to the calls and promises of Christ. See what he has already done for those of our race who relied on his grace. Look at Enoch, who walked with God; at Abraham, the friend of God; at Moses, the confidential servant of God; at Daniel, the man greatly beloved of God; at Stephen, full of faith and the Holy Ghost; at St. Paul, glowing with an ardor like that of "the rapt seraph, who adores and burns;" and at the many other worthies with whom the historian and biographer have made us acquainted. See to what heights they soared, how nearly they approached to perfection. And who enabled them to make these approaches, to soar to these heights? He, I answer, who now calls upon you to follow them; He who now offers you the same assistance which he afforded them. Rely, then, with full confidence on his perfections and promises, and recommence with new vigor your Christian warfare. Do you still hesitate and linger? O thou of little faith, wherefore dost thou doubt? Why cast round a trembling, desponding glance upon the roaring wind and stormy waves which oppose thy progress? Look rather at him who calls thee onward; at the omnipotent arm, which is to be thy strength and support. Look till you feel faith, and hope, and courage, reviving in your breast. Then say to your Lord, "I come. I will follow where thou leadest the way. I will once more aim, with renovated strength, at the perfection which I have long deemed unattainable."

This world is the place for labor, and not for rest, or enjoyment, except that enjoyment which may be found in serving God. We shall have time enough in the coming world to rest and to converse with our friends; and it may well reconcile us to separation here, if we hope to be forever with them there.

The young Christian thinks it would be best that he should be always lively, zealous, and engaged in religion; that he should feel faith, love and humility in constant exercise, and be like a flame of fire in his Master's service. But our blessed Teacher thinks otherwise. He knows that the most effectual, and, indeed, the only way, to mortify sin in our hearts, is to make us hate it; and the way to make us hate it is to suffer us to feel it. He knows that the only way to make us fervent and diligent in prayer, is to show us how many things we have to pray for, and convince us of our absolute need of his assistance. He knows that the best way to make us humble and contented is to show us what we are, and what we deserve; and that the only way to wean us from the world is, to render it a place of fatigue and uneasiness. He knows that there is nothing like the want of his presence to teach us the worth of it; and nothing like a sense of the dangerous nature of our disease, to show us the value of an Almighty Physician. Upon this plan, therefore, it is, that all his various dispensations towards Christians are conducted; and till they are acquainted with this, they cannot understand them.

CHRIST UNCHANGEABLE

As, amid all the vicissitudes of the seasons, the succession of day and night, and the changes of the weather, the sun remains and shines in the same part of the heavens; so, amid all the daily changes which the Christian experiences, from darkness to light, and from summer to winter, in both calms and tempests, the Sun of righteousness still continues the same; and 'tis the same love and wisdom which leads him to hide or to unveil his face. But the Christian is at first ready to imagine that the changes in his feelings proceed from changes in Christ; as those who do not consider the motion of the earth, fancy that the sun really rises and sets.

Above all, I would say to the Christian, never distrust the kindness, the love, the wisdom and faithfulness of your Savior; but confide in him who has promised that all things shall work together for your good. Though you may not now know what he is doing, you shall know hereafter. You will see the reason of all the trials and temptations, the dark and comfortless hours, the distressing doubts and fears, the long and tedious conflicts with which you are now exercised; and you will be convinced that not a sigh, not a tear, not a single uneasy thought was allotted you, without some wise and gracious design. Say not, then, like Jacob of old, "All these things are against me;" say not, like David, "I shall one day perish by the hand of Saul;" for all these things are for your good, and you shall never perish, neither shall any pluck you out of Christ's hand. Why should you, who are sons of the King of heaven, be lean and discontented from day to day? Remember that, if you are in the path of the just, you are the heir of God and joint heir with Christ, of an inheritance incorruptible, eternal, and that fadeth not away. Be not discouraged at the small progress you appear to make, or the difficulties you may meet with. Why should the infant be discouraged because he has not the strength of manhood, or the wisdom of age? Wait on the Lord in the diligent use of his appointed means, and he will strengthen your hearts, so that you shall mount up as on eagles' wings; you shall run, and not be weary; you shall walk, and not faint.

CHRIST A HELPER

"Who is he that walketh in darkness and hath no light? Let him trust in the name of the Lord, and stay himself upon his God" (Isa. 50:10). Let him go to Jesus, the compassionate Savior of sinners, who heals the broken in heart, who gathers the lambs in his arms, and carries them in his bosom. Go, I say, to him; tell him all your griefs and sorrows; tell him that your souls cleave to the dust; that iniquities, doubts and fears prevail against you; that you are poor, and miserable, and wretched, and blind and naked. Go to his mercy-seat, where he sits as a merciful High Priest, on purpose to give repentance and remission of sins; go and embrace his feet, lay open your whole hearts, state all your difficulties, complaints and diseases, and you will find him infinitely more gracious than you can conceive; infinitely more willing to grant your requests than you are to make them. He is love itself; 'tis his very nature to pity. Have you a hard heart? Carry it to him, and he will soften it. Have you a blind mind? He will enlighten it. Are you oppressed with a load of guilt? He will take it off. Are you defiled and polluted? He will wash you in his own blood. Have you backslidden? "Turn unto me," says he, "ye back-sliding children, and I will heal your backslidings." Come, then, to Christ, and obtain those influences of his Spirit by which you shall be enabled to grow in grace and in the knowledge of your Lord and Savior Jesus Christ. So shall your path be as the shining light, that shineth more and more unto the perfect day.

How great are the privileges which result from an ability to say, "Christ is mine!" If Christ is yours, then all that he possesses is yours. His power is yours, to defend you; his wisdom and knowledge are yours, to guide you; his righteousness is yours, to justify you; his spirit and grace are yours, to sanctify you; his heaven is yours, to receive you. He is as much yours as you are his, and as he requires all that you have to be given to him, so he gives all that he has to you. Come to him, then, with holy boldness, and take what is your own. Remember you have already received what is most difficult for him to give; his body, his blood, his life. And surely he who has given these, will not refuse you smaller blessings. You will never live happily or usefully, you will never highly enjoy or greatly adorn religion, until you can feel that Christ, and all that he possesses, are yours, and learn to come and take them as your own.

THE BIBLE ENTIRELY PRACTICAL

We may challenge any man to point out a single passage in the Bible, which does not either teach some duty, or inculcate its performance, or show the grounds on which it rests, or exhibit reasons why we should perform it. For instance; all the preceptive parts of Scripture prescribe our duty; all the invitations invite us to perform it; all the promises and threatenings are motives to its performance; all the cautions and admonitions warn us not to neglect it; the historical parts inform us what have been the consequences of neglecting and of performing it; the prophetical parts show us what these consequences will be hereafter; and the doctrinal parts show us on what grounds the whole superstructure of duty, or of practical religion, rests.

In the judgment of God there is no more heinous sin than that of hearing, with unconcern, his messages of love and mercy. "Doth not my word do good to him that walketh uprightly?" It always does. Yet Christians often go away from hearing the word unaffected.

DUTY OF STUDYING THE BIBLE

The Scriptures are given to us as a rich mine, in which we may labor, and appropriate to ourselves all the treasures we find; and the more diligently we labor, and the more wealth we obtain, so much the more is the Giver pleased. As we cannot be too careful not to pry into things secret, so we cannot be too diligent in searching into every thing which God has revealed. And if we search in the manner which he has prescribed, we shall make all the good things contained in the Scriptures our own in a still higher sense. We shall make that God, that Savior, that holiness, that heaven, which the Bible reveals, our own forever, our own to possess and to enjoy. In short, every truth which it reveals is ours to enlighten us; every precept is ours to direct us; every admonition is ours to warn us; every promise is ours to encourage and animate us. For these purposes God has given, and for these purposes we are to receive them.

PRAYER

We may judge of the state of our hearts by the earnestness of our prayers. You cannot make a rich man beg like a poor man; you cannot make a man that is full cry for food like one that is hungry: no more will a man who has a good opinion of himself, cry for mercy like one who feels that he is poor and needy.

The symptoms of spiritual decline are like those which attend the decay of bodily health. It generally commences with loss of appetite, and a disrelish for spiritual food, prayer, reading the Scriptures, and devotional books. Whenever you perceive these symptoms, be alarmed, for your spiritual health is in danger; apply immediately to the great Physician for a cure.

The best means of keeping near to God is the prayer closet. Here the battle is won or lost.

If a man begins to be impatient because his prayers for any blessings are not answered, it is a certain proof, that a self-righteous dependence on his own merits prevails in his heart to a great extent; for the language of impatience is, "I deserve the blessing: I had a right to expect that it would be bestowed, and it ought to have been bestowed ere this." It is evident that a man who feels that he deserves nothing, will never be impatient because he receives nothing; but will say, "I have nothing to complain of, I receive as much as I deserve." Again, when a man wonders, or thinks it strange, that he does not receive a blessing for which he has prayed, it shows that he relies on his own merits. The language of such feelings is, "It is very strange that I, who have prayed so well, and so long, and had so much reason to expect a blessing do not receive it." Persons who feel truly humble, on the contrary, are surprised, not when blessings are withheld, but when they are bestowed. It appears very strange and wonderful to them that God should bestow any favors on creatures, so unworthy as themselves, or pay any regard to prayers so polluted as their own. This is the temper to which every person must be brought before God will answer his prayers.

PRAISE

No one needs to be told, that the surest method to obtain new favors from an earthly benefactor, is to be thankful for those which he has already bestowed. It is the same with respect to our heavenly Benefactor. Praise and thanksgiving are even more prevalent than sacrifices or prayers. I have somewhere met with an account of a Christian, who was shipwrecked upon a desolate island, while all his companions perished in the waves. In this situation, he spent many days in fasting and prayer, that God would open a way for his deliverance; but his prayers received no answer. At length, musing on the goodness of God, in preserving him from the dangers of the sea, he resolved to spend a day in thanksgiving and praise, for this and other favors. Before the conclusion of the day, a vessel arrived, and restored him in safety to his country and friends. Another instance, equally in point, we find in the history of Solomon. At the dedication of the temple, many prayers were made, and many sacrifices offered, without any token of the divine acceptance. But when singers and players on instruments began as one to make one sound to be heard, in praising and thanking the Lord, saying, "For he is good, for his mercy endureth forever;" then the glory of the Lord descended and filled the temple. The reason why praise and thanksgiving are thus prevalent with God, is, that they, above all other duties, glorify Him. "Whoso offereth praise," says he, "glorifieth me;" and those who thus honor him, he will honor (1 Sam. 2:30).

THE LORD'S SUPPER

At the communion table we are in fact assembled to attend our Savior's funeral, to look at his dead body, as we look at the countenance of a deceased friend before the coffin is closed. And if every wrong, every worldly feeling should die away, while we are contemplating the corpse of a friend, how much more ought this to be the case, when this friend is Christ! I think it may be profitable sometimes to shut ourselves up in imagination, in our Savior's tomb, and feel as if he were there buried with us.

At the table of our Lord, each of us should recollect the personal favors and marks of kindness, which he has himself received from Christ, or through his mediation. Our temporal mercies, our spiritual privileges should all pass in review. We should look back to the never to be forgotten time of love, when he found us poor, miserable, wretched, blind and naked; dead in trespasses and sins, having no hope, and without God in the world. We should remember how he pitied us, awakened us, convinced us of sin, and drew us to himself by the cords of love. We should remember how often he has since healed our backslidings, pardoned our sins, borne with our unbelief, ingratitude, and slowness to learn; supplied our wants, listened to our complaints, alleviated our sorrows, and revived our drooping spirits when we were ready to faint. In short, we must remember all the way by which he has led us, these many years, through a wilderness of sins, sorrows, trials and temptations. Thus we shall be convinced that no sickly infant ever cost its mother a thousandth part of the care, and labor, and suffering, which we have cost our Savior; and that no mother has ever shown her infant a thousandth part of the watchful tenderness, which our Savior has shown to us.

Was Christ a man of sorrows, and acquainted with grief? Then, Christians, we need not be surprised or offended, if we are often called to drink of the cup of sorrows; if we find this world a vale of tears. This is one of the ways in which we must be conformed to our glorious Head. Indeed, his example has sanctified grief, and almost rendered it pleasant to mourn. One would think that

Christians could scarcely wish to go rejoicing through a world, which their Master passed through mourning. The paths in which we follow him are bedewed with his tears, and stained with his blood. It is true, that from the ground thus watered and fertilized, many rich flowers and fruits of paradise spring up to refresh us, in which we may, and ought to rejoice. But still our joy should be softened and sanctified by godly sorrow. When we are partaking of the feast which his love has spread for us, we should never forget how dearly it was purchased.

> *"There's not a gift his hand bestows*
> *But cost his heart a groan."*

The joy, the honor, the glory, through eternity, shall be ours; but the sorrows, the sufferings, the agonies which purchased it, were all his own.

RELATIVE DUTIES OF CHRISTIANS

Since all Christians are members of the same body, they ought not to envy each other. What could be more absurd than for the eye to envy the dexterity of the hand, or the feet to envy the perspicuity of the eye which directed their motions, and prevented them from running into danger? Still more absurd is it, if possible, for one Christian to envy the gifts, or graces, or usefulness of another, since the whole body, and he amongst the rest, enjoys the benefit of them. The fact is, whenever God bestows a favor on any Christian, he does, in effect, confer a favor on all; just as when a man heals, or clothes one part of the body, he confers a benefit on the whole. Rejoice, and bless God, then, Christians, when he honors or favors any fellow

Christian, for it is an act of kindness done to you, and will promote your present and eternal felicity.

No Christian should be dissatisfied with his lot if poor and despised, or indulge pride if honored and prospered. Every one is in that place which infinite wisdom sees best for him, and the most highly favored Christians are, in many respects, dependent on the lowest. The eye cannot say to the hand, I have no need of you. If the whole body were an eye, where were the hearing? And if the whole body were hearing, where were the smelling? But now God hath set the members in the body, every one as it hath pleased him, and it is the same in the great body of Christ.

It is incumbent on every Christian to ascertain for what he is qualified, and what service he is called to perform, for the body of which he is a member. You can easily conceive what would be the consequence, in the human body, should the feet attempt to perform the work of the hands, or the hands, the office of the eye. Almost equally pernicious and ridiculous are the consequences occasioned by the self-ignorance, vanity, or false modesty of many Christians. They either do not know their place, or if they do, will not perform the duties of it. Hence some will attempt to perform the duty of social prayer, or of exhortation, or of expounding the Scriptures, whom God never designed, and therefore never qualified for that work, and who, of course, cannot perform it in an edifying, acceptable manner; while others, whom he had thus qualified, for some cause or other, decline attempting it. Hence it is too often the case, that a church of Christ, instead of resembling a well-organized body in which the several members know and keep their place, and perform its duties, resembles a disorderly family, in which no one knows his employment, and, of course, there is nothing but confusion and complaint.

LOVE ONE ANOTHER

There are some Christians whom it is not very easy to love, on account of some disagreeable peculiarities about them; but we shall love them hereafter, as we love our own souls, and they will love us, in a similar manner. Besides, our Savior loves them, notwithstanding all these imperfections; and ought not our affections to follow his? If he were now visibly on earth, and we were permitted to stand by his side, if we saw him direct a look of love on any individual, would not our affections immediately flow out towards that person, however disagreeable or imperfect he might be? Such a look our Savior does direct on the most unlovely of his disciples. Let us, then, love them all, for his sake.

UNIVERSAL LAW OF BENEVOLENCE

"Not for ourselves, but others;" is the grand law of nature, inscribed by the hand of God on every part of creation. Not for itself, but others, does the sun dispense its beams; not for themselves, but others, do the clouds distill their showers; not for herself, but others, does the earth unlock her treasures; not for themselves, but others, do the trees produce their fruits, or the flowers diffuse their fragrance and display their various hues. So, not for himself, but others, are the blessings of Heaven bestowed on man; and whenever, instead of diffusing them around, he devotes them exclusively to his own gratification, and shuts himself up in the dark and flinty caverns of selfishness, he transgresses the great law of creation; he cuts himself off from the created universe, and its Author; he sacrilegiously converts to his own use the favors which were given him for the relief of others, and must be considered, not only as an unprofitable, but as a fraudulent servant, who has worse than wasted his Lord's money. He, who thus lives only to himself, and consumes the bounty of Heaven upon his lusts, or consecrates it to the demon of avarice, is a barren rock in a fertile plain; he is a thorny bramble in a fruitful vineyard; he is the grave of God's blessings; he is the very Arabian Desert of the moral world. And if he is highly exalted in wealth or power, he stands, inaccessible and strong, like an insulated towering cliff, which exhibits only a cold and cheerless prospect, intercepts the genial beams of the sun, chills the vales below with its gloomy shade, adds fresh keenness to the freezing blast, and tempts down the lightnings of an angry heaven. How different this from the gently rising hill, clothed to its summit with fruits and flowers, which attracts and receives the dews of heaven, and retaining only sufficient to supply its numerous offspring, sends the remainder in a thousand streams to bless the vales which lie at its feet!

DUTIES TO THE HEATHEN

It is a fact that vigorous and persevering exertions in favor of religion abroad, naturally excite, and are inseparably connected with similar and successful exertions at home. Witness the example of Great Britain. While she was reaching the full cup of life and salvation to other countries, the drops which fell from it refreshed and fertilized her own. Witness the present religious situation of our own country. Never, in the same space of time, was so much done for its amelioration; never were the Scriptures so generally diffused among us; never were our domestic missions in so prosperous a state; never were their endeavors crowned with so much success, as since we began to send Bibles and missionaries to the heathen. God has been pouring out spiritual blessings upon our churches, our towns, our villages and our schools; and thus, for every missionary whom we have sent abroad, he has given us ten to labor at home. If we wish to obtain greater blessings of a similar kind, we must seek them in a similar way. If vice and infidelity are to be finally conquered, and banished from our country, the battle must be fought, and the victory won, on the plains of India.

True charity receives her instructions, as well as her existence, from faith in God's word; and when faith points to human beings in danger, charity, without delaying to propose questions, hastens to their relief.

Our houses are built, our vineyards are planted, around the base of a volcano. They may be fair and flourishing today, while tomorrow ashes may be all that remains. Open your hands wide, then, while they contain any blessings to bestow; for of that which you give you can never be deprived.

SEE THAT YOU ABOUND IN THIS GRACE ALSO

Unless we strenuously aim at universal holiness, we can have no satisfactory evidence, that we are the servants of Christ. A servant of Christ is one that obeys Christ as his Master, and makes Christ's revealed word the rule of his conduct. No man, then, can have any evidence that he is a servant of Christ any further than he obeys the will of Christ. And no man can have any evidence that he obeys the will of Christ in one particular, unless he sincerely and strenuously aims to obey in every particular; for the will of Christ is one.

In consequence of their natural constitution, of the circumstances in which they are placed, or of the absence of temptation, most Christians find it comparatively easy to avoid some sins, to be exemplary in the performance of some duties, and to cultivate some branches of the Christian temper with success. One man, for instance, enjoys much leisure and has a taste for study; hence the acquisition of religious knowledge becomes easy to him. Another is blessed with a mild and amiable disposition, and of course can regulate his temper without much difficulty. A third is constitutionally liberal, and can therefore contribute readily to religious and charitable objects. A fourth is quiet and retiring, and is for this reason little tempted to pride, ambition, or discontent. A fifth is naturally bold and ardent. Of course, he can easily overcome indolence and the fear of man. In a word, there are a very few Christians, who, for these and other similar reasons, do not in some respects excel. But the evil is that they are prone, though perhaps without being sensible of it, to attach an undue importance to that grace or duty in which they excel, to make the whole of religion to consist in it, and to neglect other things of equal importance, the performance of which they would find more difficult. Nay, more; they secretly regard the eminence which they have attained in some respects, as an excuse for great deficiencies in others; and endeavor to atone for a neglect of self-denying duties, by attending with peculiar zeal to those duties which are more easy.

One man, for instance, is lukewarm in his affections, formal in his devotions, and makes little progress in subduing his sinful propensities. But he comforts himself with the hope that his knowledge of religious truth is increasing. Another, who neglects to improve opportunities for acquiring religious knowledge, derives consolation from the warmth of his zeal, and the liveliness of his affections. One person is by no means disposed to contribute liberally for the promotion of Christ's cause and the relief of the poor; but he hopes to atone for his deficiency in this respect, by the frequency and fervency of his prayers. Another neglects prayer, meditation and communion with God, but he quiets himself by pleading the pressure of worldly business, and by liberal contributions for religious and charitable purposes. Thus, as there are few Christians who do not excel in some respects, there are few who are not, in some respects, exceedingly deficient. Small indeed is the number of those who sedulously strive to stand perfect and complete in all the will of God.

Nothing is more common than to meet with Christians who in many respects are eminently and exemplarily pious, but who, by some sinful imprudence or defect, render their characters vulnerable, destroy all the good effects of their example, and dishonor instead of adorning religion. They resemble a beautiful and well-proportioned body, which has been disfigured by a wound, or which has lost a limb, or some member of which is disproportionately large. While in some respects they are giants, in others they are mere dwarfs. Hence not only their reputation, but their influence, their comfort, their usefulness are impaired, and they adorn religion less than many others who are in many respects greatly their inferiors, but who are more uniform and consistent in their conduct.

Christ commands us, whether we eat or drink, or whatever we do, to do all to the glory of God. Perhaps some will ask,

"How is this possible? We cannot be always thinking of God; we must attend to our business, provide for our own wants and those of our families." True; but look at a man about to send a ship to a foreign port. As he purchases his cargo, and makes the requisite preparations, he considers what articles are most suitable for the market; what provisions most necessary for the voyage; how the ship is to be rigged and manned; in short, all his plans are laid with reference to the end of the voyage. So the Christian, though not always thinking of heaven, should take care that all his business and all his pleasures may forward his journey thither, and promote his great object of preparation for that abode of blessedness.

CHRIST GLORIFIED IN HIS CHURCH

When we look at the sun, we only perceive that it is a bright and glorious luminary. But when we behold the earth in spring, in summer or autumn, clothed with luxuriant vegetation, adorned with flowers, and enlivened by myriads of sportive, happy beings; when we compare this state of things with the rigors, the frost, the barrenness of winter, recollect that the sun is, instrumentally, the cause of this mighty difference, and reflect how gloomy and desolate our world would be, if wholly deprived of its beams; we have far more clear and enlarged conceptions of the value and excellence of this luminary. The sun is then, if I may so express it, glorified in the earth, and admired in all the productions and beneficial effects which result from his influence. In a similar manner will Christ, the Son of righteousness, be glorified and admired in his people. It will then be clearly seen how much mercy was necessary to pardon their sins, how much grace was required to sanctify, preserve and glorify them; how much wisdom, goodness and power were displayed in devising and executing the wondrous plan of their redemption. They will not, therefore, be admired, but Christ will be seen and admired in them. The assembled universe will be ready to exclaim, with one voice, How infinitely powerful, wise, and good must he be, who could transform sinful, guilty worms of the dust, into beings so perfectly glorious and lovely!

MISCELLANEOUS DIRECTIONS TO CHRISTIANS

God commands all men to repent. Christians have enough to repent of daily; and if they are not in a penitent frame, they justify impenitent sinners.

Let your great Physician heal you in his own way. Only follow his directions and take the medicine which he prescribes, and then quietly leave the result with him.

What God calls a man to do, He will carry him through. I would undertake to govern half a dozen worlds, if God called me to do it; but I would not undertake to govern half a dozen sheep unless God called me to it.

To a person who has been frustrated in a benevolent design: "I congratulate you, and anticipate your eventual success. I do not recollect ever to have succeeded in anything of importance, in which I did not meet with some rebuff, at the commencement."

Suppose you were to pass over a pit which had no bottom; would you endeavor to fill it up, or bridge it over? Consider this image well, and it will cure a covetous spirit.

Anticipated sorrows are harder to bear than real ones, because Christ does not support us under them. In every slough we may see the footsteps of Christ's flock who have gone before us.

Christian friends, when separated from each other's society, may derive comfort from the reflection, that God is able to extend a hand to two of his children at the same time, however remote may be their places of habitation.

Everything we do or say should be immediately tried by a little court within our own breast. Our motives should be examined, and a decision made on the spot.

Our best rule is, to give God the same place in our hearts, that He holds in the universe. We must make Him all in all. We should act as if there were no beings in the universe but God and ourselves.

As the eye which has gazed at the sun, cannot immediately discern any other object; as the man who has been accustomed to behold the ocean, turns with contempt from a stagnant pool, so the mind which has contemplated eternity, overlooks and despises the things of time.

If at any time you have enlargement in prayer and are favored with access to the throne of grace, do not go away satisfied and self-complacent. Pride says, "I have done very well now; God will accept this." You perhaps discover that this is the suggestion of pride; it then takes a new turn. Another would not have discovered it to be pride; I must be very humble to see it thus. Thus if you continue the search, you will find pride, like the different coats of an onion, lurking one beneath another to the very center.

Praise Christ for everything. He is the foundation of every good thought, desire and affection. It should be our aim to draw all we can from him by prayer, and return him all we can by praise.

O DEATH! WHERE IS THY STING?

The power of death, the last enemy, is destroyed, as it respects all who believe in Christ. Instead of being the jailer of hell and the grave, he is now, as it respects Christ's people, the porter of paradise. All he can now do is to cause them to sleep in Jesus, release their immortal spirits from the fetters which bind them to earth, and deposit their weary bodies in the tomb, as a place of rest, till Christ comes at the last day, to raise them incorruptible, glorious and immortal; and reunite them to their souls in a state of perfect, never-ending felicity.

TO THE MINISTERS OF CHRIST

Every benevolent person is gratified by being made the bearer of pleasing intelligence. The messenger, who is commissioned to open the prison doors of an insolvent debtor, or pardoned criminal, and restore him to the embraces of his family; the officer, who is sent by commander in chief to carry home tidings of an important victory; and still more the ambassador, who is appointed to proclaim pardon and peace, in his sovereign's name, to conquered rebels; thinks himself, and is thought by others, to have received no common favor. Should God put into your hands the wonder-working rod of Moses; should he commission and enable you to work miracles of beneficence, to enrich the poor, to comfort the miserable, to restore sight to the blind, hearing to the deaf, health to the diseased, and life to the dead; you would esteem it a favor and honor, incomparably greater than earthly monarchs can bestow. But in committing the gospel to your care, God has conferred on you honors and favors, compared with which, even the power of working miracles is a trifle. He has put into your hands the cross of Christ, an instrument of far greater efficacy than the rod of Moses. He has sent you to proclaim the most joyful tidings that heaven can desire, or that earth can hear. He has sent you to preach deliverance to captives, the recovery of sight to the blind, the balm of Gilead and the great Physician to the spiritually wounded and diseased, salvation to the self-destroyed, and everlasting life to the dead. In a word, he commissions and enables them to work miracles, not upon the bodies, but upon the souls of men; miracles not merely of power, but of grace and mercy; miracles, to perform which, an angel would think himself highly honored, in being sent down from heaven; miracles from the performance of which it is difficult to say whether greater glory redounds to God, or greater happiness to man. Well then may every minister of Christ exclaim with Paul, I thank my God for that he counted me faithful, putting me into the ministry.

Oh, if ministers only saw the inconceivable glory that is before them, and the preciousness of Christ, they would not be able to refrain from going about, leaping and clapping their hands for joy, and exclaiming, "I'm a minister of Christ! I'm a minister of Christ!"

Although, in committing the gospel to their trust, God has conferred on ministers the greatest honor and favor which can be given to mortals, yet, like all other favors, it brings with it a great increase of responsibility. Remember that the more highly anyone is exalted, in this respect, the more difficult it becomes to stand, and the more dangerous it is to fall. He who falls from a pulpit seldom stops short of the lowest abyss in hell.

HAPPINESS OF HEAVEN

Only to be permitted to contemplate such a being as Jehovah, to see goodness, holiness, justice, mercy, long-suffering and sovereignty personified and condensed; to see them united with eternity, infinite power, unerring wisdom, omnipresence and all sufficiency; to see all these natural and moral perfections indissolubly united and blended in sweet harmony in a pure, spiritual being, and that being placed on the throne of the universe; I say to see this would be happiness enough to fill the mind of any creature in existence. But in addition to this, to have this ineffable being for our God, our portion, our all; to be permitted to say, "This God is our God forever and ever;" to have his resplendent countenance smile upon us; to be encircled in his everlasting arms of power, and faithfulness, and love, to hear his voice saying to us, "I am yours, and you are mine; nothing shall every pluck you from my hands, or separate you from my love, but you shall be with me where I am, behold my glory, and live to reign with me forever and ever;" this is too much; it is honor, it is glory, it is happiness too overwhelming, too transporting for mortal minds to conceive, or for mortal frames to support; and it is perhaps well for us that here we know but in part, and that it doth not yet appear what we shall be. O then, in all circumstances, under all inward and outward afflictions, let God's Israel rejoice in their Creator, let the children of Zion be joyful in their King.

You have, doubtless, often observed that when your minds have been intently and pleasingly occupied, you have become almost unconscious of the flight of time; minutes and hours have flown away, with, apparently, unusual swiftness, and the setting or rising sun has surprised you, long before you expected its approach. But in heaven, the saints will be entirely lost and swallowed up in God; and their minds will be so completely absorbed in the contemplation of his ineffable, infinite, uncreated, glories, that they will be totally unconscious how time, or, rather, how eternity passes; and not only years, but millions of ages, such as we call ages, will be flown ere they are aware. Thus, a thousand years will seem to them but as one day, and yet so great, so ecstatic will be their happiness, that one day will be as a thousand years. And as there will be nothing to interrupt them, no bodily wants to call off their attention, no weariness to compel them to rest, no vicissitude of seasons or of day and night to disturb their contemplations; it is more than possible that innumerable ages may pass away, before they think of asking how long they have been in heaven, or even before they are conscious that a single hour has elapsed.

How often, Christians, have your hearts been made to burn with love, and gratitude, and admiration, and joy, while Christ has opened to you the Scriptures, and caused you to know a little of that love which passeth knowledge! How often has one transient glimpse of the light of God's countenance turned your night into day, banished your sorrows, supported you under heavy afflictions, and caused you to rejoice with joy unspeakable and full of glory! Oh, then, what must it be to escape forever from error, and ignorance, and darkness, and sin, into the region of bright, unclouded, eternal day; to see your God and Redeemer, face to face; continually to contemplate, with immortal strength, glories so dazzlingly bright, that one moment's view of them would now, like a stream of lightning, turn your frail bodies into dust; to see the eternal volume of the divine counsels, the mighty map of the divine mind; unfolded to your eager, piercing gaze; to explore the heights and depths, the lengths and breadths of the Redeemer's love, and still to see new wonders, glories and beauties pouring upon your minds, in constant, endless succession, calling forth new songs of praise; -songs in which you will unite, not, as now, with mortal companions and mortal voices, but with the innumerable choir of angels, with the countless myriads of the redeemed, all shouting with a voice like the voice of many waters, "Alleluia, for the Lord God omnipotent reigneth!"

****

ANECDOTES EXTRACTED FROM A MAGAZINE

One day, he went to visit a mother, who was disconsolate from the loss of a child. He said to her as follows: "Suppose, now, some one was making a beautiful crown for your to wear; and you knew it was for you, and that you were to receive it and wear it as soon as it should be done. Now, if the maker of it were to come, and, in order to make the crown more beautiful and splendid, were to take some of your jewels, to put into it; should you be sorrowful and unhappy, because they were taken away for a little while, when you knew they were gone to make up your crown?"

The mother said, that no one could conceive of the relief, the soothing, quieting influence which this comparison had on her mind.

On another occasion he went to see a sick person, who was very much troubled, because she could not keep her mind all the time upon Christ, on account of the distracting influences of her sufferings, and the various objects and occurrences of the sick room, which constantly called off her attention. She was afraid she did not love her Savior, as she found it so difficult to fix her mind upon him. Dr. Payson said, "Suppose you were to see a little sick child, lying in its mother's lap, with its faculties impaired by its sufferings, so that it was, generally, in a troubled sleep; but now and then it just opens its eyes a little, and gets a glimpse of its mother's face, so as to be recalled to the recollection that it is in its mother's arms; and suppose that always, at such a time, it should smile faintly with evident pleasure to find where it was; should you doubt whether that child loved its mother or not?"

The poor sufferer's doubts and despondency were gone in a moment.

A gentlemen, who saw and conversed with Dr. Payson in Boston, when he visited this city, towards the latter part of his life, was led, by his preaching and conversation, to a considerable degree of serious concern for his soul. The man's wife was still in a great measure indifferent to the subject. One day, meeting her in company, he said to her: "Madam, I think your husband is looking upwards, and making some effort to rise above this world, toward God and heaven. You must not let him try alone. Whenever I see the husband struggling alone in such efforts, it makes me think of a dove, endeavoring to fly upwards, while it has one broken wing. It leaps and flutters, and perhaps raises itself a little way, and then it becomes wearied, and drops back again to the ground. If both wings cooperate, then it mounts easily."

A LETTER TO HIS WIFE BEFORE MARRIAGE

When I wrote my first letter after my late visit, I felt almost angry with you and quite so with myself. And why angry with you? Because I began to fear you would prove a dangerous rival to my Lord and Master, and draw away my heart from His service. My Louisa, should this be the case, I should certainly hate you. I am Christ's; I must be Christ's; He has purchased me dearly, and I should hate the mother who bore me, if she proved even the *innocent* occasion of drawing me from Him. I feared that you would do this. For a little time the conflict of my feelings was dreadful beyond description. For a few moments I wished I had never seen you. Had you been a right hand, or a right eye, had you been the lifeblood in my veins (and you are dear to me as either) I must have given you up, had I continued to feel as I did. But blessed be God, He has shown me my weakness only to strengthen me. I now feel very differently. I still love you dearly as ever, but my love leads me *to* Christ and not *from* Him.

A LETTER TO HIS WIFE AFTER THEIR MARRIAGE

The prospects on the banks of the river were delightful and cheering every moment. The day was fine and the swiftness of our motion was agreeable, and, to crown all, I saw God in his works, and tasted his goodness in everything. I thought of you almost every moment, and nothing but the presence of yourself and the children was wanting to make me as happy as I could be in this world. Every one on board is in a bustle, and I am standing away in one corner talking with my best, dearest earthly friend. You, at the distance of five hundred miles, have more attractions for me than the whole city of Philadelphia, which is spread out before me. Kiss the children for me, talk to them about me; love me as I do you. I love you far better than I did when I wrote the last letter to you before our marriage.

AN EXAMPLE OF HIS DOMESTIC INFLUENCE

Referring to Elizabeth Payson Prentiss, we are told,
"By far the strongest of all the impressions of her childhood related to her father. His presence was to her the
happiest spot on earth, and any special expression of his
affection would throw her into an ecstasy of delight. When
he was away she pined for his return. 'The children all send
a great deal of love, and Elizabeth says, Do tell Papa to
come home,' wrote her mother to him, when she was six
years old. Her recollections of her father were singularly
vivid. She could describe minutely his domestic habits,
how he looked and talked as he sat by the fireside or at the
table, his delight in and skillful use of carpenters' tools, his
ingenious devices for amusing her and diverting his own
weariness as he lay sick in bed, *e.g.,* tearing up sheets of
white paper into tiny bits, and then letting her pour them
out of the window to 'make believe it snowed,' or counting
all the bristles in a clothes-brush, and then as she came in
from school, holding it up and bidding her guess their
number; his coolness and efficiency in the wild excitements
of a conflagration, the calm deliberation with which he
walked past the horror-stricken onlookers and cut the rope
by which a suicide was suspended; these and other
incidents she would recall a third of a century after his
death, as if she had just heard of or just witnessed them. To
her child's imagination his memory seemed to be invested
with the triple halo of father, hero, and saint. A little
picture of him was always near her. She never mentioned
his name without tender affection and reverence. Nor is
this at all strange. She was almost nine years old when he
died; and his influence, during these years, penetrated to
her inmost being.

She once said that of her father's virtues one only, punctuality, had descended to her. But here she was surely wrong. Not only did she owe to him some of the most striking peculiarities of her physical and mental constitution, but her piety itself, if not inherited, was largely inspired and shaped by his. In the whole tone and expression of her earlier religious life, at least, one sees him clearly reflected. His devotional habits, in particular, left upon her an indelible impression. Once, when four or five years old, she came rushing by mistake into his room, she found him prostrate on his face, completely lost in prayer. A short time before her death, speaking of this scene to a friend, she remarked that the remembrance of it had influenced her ever since. What somebody said of Sara Coleridge might indeed have been said with no less truth of Elizabeth Payson: 'Her father had looked down into her eyes and left in them the light of his own.'"
(*"More Love to Thee,"* Calvary Press, pp. 11,12)

A LETTER TO HIS MOTHER EARLY IN MINISTRY

I have sometimes heard of spells and charms to excite love, and have wished for them, when a boy, that I might cause others to love me. But how much do I now wish for some charm which should lead men to love the Savior! Could I paint a true likeness of Him, methinks I should rejoice to hold it up to the view and admiration of all creation, and be hid behind it forever. It would be heaven enough to hear Him praised and adored. But I can not paint Him; I can not describe Him; I can not make others love Him; nay. I can not love Him a thousandth part so much as I ought to myself. O, for an angel's tongue! O, for the tongues of ten thousand angels, to sound His praises.

PERSONAL RESOLUTIONS HE ADOPTED

In his frequent seasons of illness, and his multiplied public engagements, he saw cause of danger that his private devotions would suffer interruption or abatement. To guard against such an evil, appears to have been one object of the following resolutions, which were adopted, or renewed, near the close of one year. While they are not as detailed as those adopted by Jonathan Edwards, they, nonetheless demonstrate the deep seriousness which drove him to seek to live always for the glory of God.

"1. I will, on no pretense whatever, omit reading the Scriptures, with prayer, morning and evening.

2. When practicable, I will spend one day in every week in fasting and prayer.

3. I will allow six hours for sleep.

4. I will endeavor to redeem the time by being diligent and fervent in business.

5. I will live more to the glory of God than I have done.

6. I will, every evening, review my conduct through the day, and see how far I have fulfilled these resolutions."

HIS RULE REGARDING PASTORAL VISITS

My rule, in regard to visiting, is to visit as much as time and health will permit. I make none but pastoral visits. I gave my people to understand, when I was settled (as their minister), that they must not invite me to dine or sup when they did not wish to have the conversation turn wholly on religious subjects. This has saved me much time and trouble.

BOOKS HE FOUND MOST USEFUL TO HIS SOUL

The books which I have found most useful to me are Jonathan Edward's Works, David Brainard's Life, John Newton's Letters, John Owen's Treatise on Indwelling Sin, Mortification of Sin in Believers, and the 130th Psalm, and Thomas a Kempis's Imitation of Christ, trans- lated by Payne; for Stanhope's translation I think not so good. If you have not seen Thomas a Kempis, I beg you to procure it. Some things you will not like; but, for spiritu- ality and weanedness from the world, I know of nothing equal to it. Perhaps I ought to include, in the above list, Richard Baxter's Reformed Pastor, and Saint's Everlasting Rest.

A FELLOW MINISTER'S DESCRIPTION
OF THE POWER OF PAYSON'S PRAYERS

"No one can form an adequate conception of what Dr. Payson was from any of the productions of his pen. Admirable as his written sermons are, his extempore prayers and the gushings of his heart in familiar talk were altogether higher and more touching than anything he wrote. It was my custom to close my eyes when he began to pray, and it was always a letting down, a sort of rude fall to open them again, when he had concluded, and find myself still on earth. His prayers always took my spirit into the immediate presence of Christ; amid the glories of the spiritual world; and to look round again on this familiar and comparatively misty earth was almost painful. At every prayer I heard him offer, during the seven years in which he was my spiritual guide, I never ceased to feel new astonishment, at the wonderful variety and depth and richness and even novelty of feeling and expression which were poured forth. This was a feeling with which every hearer sympathized, and it is a fact well-known, that Christians trained under his influence were generally remarkable for their devotional habits." (Calvin E. Stowe)

AN ADDRESS DELIVERED TO SEAMAN
(Preached at the opening of the Portland Marine Bible Society)

This sermon, or address, was perhaps the most popular of the productions of his pen. Although never intended for the press, it was taken up and read the world over. His biographer states, "Its popularity, from the very first, has been unrivaled by anything of its kind. Copies of it have multiplied to an extent past computation. It has been translated into some of the languages of the old world, and pretty extensively circulated on the coasts of the Mediterranean, from the press at Malta."

In a letter that he wrote to his mother the following month, he tells her,

"My Address to Seamen is published, and I shall send you one with this letter. They have printed nine thousand copies; three thousand in the sermon form, and six thousand in the form of a tract. They intend to send them to every seaport in the United States. I know you will pray that a blessing may go with it. It produced a great effect upon seaman and others for a time; but I do not know that any have been really awakened by it. One hundred and forty sailors applied, the next day, for Bibles, most of whom paid for them. I could not but wonder to see God work by it. I had only ten days' notice, and, during that time, had to prepare and preach six sermons, besides the Address, and another sermon which I did not preach."

We rejoice, my seafaring friends, to see so many of you assembled here, on this occasion. Most cordially do we bid you welcome, a thousand times welcome to the temple of

Him, who is no less your God than ours. Welcome, welcome, weary, weather-beaten sailor, to the place where rest is offered to the weary in the name of Jesus Christ. For you this place is now opened. For you this Bible Society was formed. For you this meeting was appointed. For you our united prayers have now ascended before the mercy seat of Heaven. You it is, whom, as friends and brothers, the speaker now purposes to address.

And why does he address you? Why have we invited and welcomed you here this evening? Because you are our fellow-creatures, our fellow-immortals. Because you are our shipmates in the great ship of this world; and are sailing with us to the shores of eternity. Because you have something within you which thinks and feels; and that something is an immortal soul; a soul worth infinitely more than all the merchandise, which you ever assisted in conveying across the seas; a soul worth more than all the stars which twinkle above you, while keeping your evening watch on deck; a soul which will continue to live, and to be happy or miserable, when all those stars are quenched in everlasting night. Yes, mark me, shipmates, you have, each, such a soul within you; a soul dear to Him who made it; a soul, for whose salvation Jesus Christ shed his blood; and for the loss of which, the whole world, could you gain it, would be no compensation. This precious freight, these immortal souls, are embarked in frail vessels, on the dangerous voyage of life; a voyage which you are even now pursuing, and which will terminate, either in the Port of Heaven, or in the Gulf of Perdition. To one or the other of these places you are all bound. In one or the other of them, you will all land at death. In which of them you shall land will depend on the course you steer. These are the reasons why we feel concerned for you; why we address you. We wish you to steer a safe course. We know there is but one such course. We wish you to make sure of a good harbor, in which you may rest quietly after the toilsome voyage of life is ended. We know there is but one such harbor. We know that this harbor is not easy to find. We know that the sea over which you sail is full of sunken rocks and quicksands, on which many a brother sailor has made shipwreck of his soul. Your voyage is, therefore, exceedingly dangerous. We meet you pursuing this voyage and wish to speak you. When you speak to a vessel, one of the first questions you ask her is, "Where are you bound?" Allow me to ask the same question.

Ho, there, creature of God, immortal spirit, voyager to Eternity! Whither art thou bound? Heard I the answer aright? Was it, "I don't know!" Not know where you are bound! Heard you ever such an answer to this question before? Should you hear such an answer from a spoken vessel, would you not conclude its crew to be either drunk or mad? and would you not soon expect to hear of its loss? Not know where you are bound! And have you then, for so many years, been beating about in the fogs of ignorance and uncertainty; with no port in view; the sport of storms and currents; driven hither and thither as the winds change, without any hope of ever making a harbor, and liable, every moment, to strike upon a lee shore? Not know where you are bound! Alas, then, I fear you are bound to the Gulf of Perdition; and that you will be driven on the rocks of Despair, which are now right ahead of you, and which, sooner or later, bring up all, who know not where they are bound, and who care not what course they steer. If I have taken my observation correctly, you are in the Lee Current, which sets directly into a Gulf where you will find no bottom with a thousand fathoms of line. Not know where you are bound! You must then be in distress. You have either removed your rudder, or you have no compass, chart, or quadrant on board; nor any pilot who can carry you into the port of Heaven.

And what pilot, you will perhaps ask in reply, can carry us there? Who can tell us, with certainty, that there is any such port? On what chart is it laid down? And how do we know, how do you know, how can any man know, that what you have now told us is true?

These are fair questions, shipmates, and you shall have an answer; but allow me, first to ask you a few questions. Should you see a fine ship, well built, handsomely rigged, and completely equipped for a voyage, could any man make you believe that she built herself? or that she was built by chance? or that she sprung, like a bubble, out of the sea? Would you not feel as certain, that she was the work of some builder, as if you had stood by, and seen him shape every timber, and drive every bolt? And can you, then, believe, that this great ship, the world, built itself? or that it was built by chance? or that it sprung out of nothing without any cause? Do you not feel as certain, that it was made by some great, and wise, and powerful builder, as if you had stood by and seen him make it? Yes, you will say, every ship is built by some man; but he that built all things must be more than man: he must be God.

Another question. Should you see a vessel go every year, for many years successively to a distant port, and return at a set time; performing all her voyages with perfect regularity, and never going a cable's length out of her course, nor being a day out of her time, could you be made to believe that she had no commander, pilot, or helmsman on board; that she went and came of her own accord; or that she had nothing to steer her but the wind? Would you have any more doubt that she was under the command of some skillful navigator, than if you were on board, and saw him? Look then, once more, at this great ship, the world.

See how regularly she makes her annual voyage round the sun, without ever getting out of her course, or being a day out of her time. Should she gain or lose a single day in making this voyage, what would all your nautical Tables be good for? Now, would she go and come with such perfect regularity and exactness of her own accord? or with no one to regulate her course? Can you any more doubt that she is under the direction of some skillful commander, than if you saw him regulating all her motions? But if the world has a pilot, a commander, who is he? Ay, shipmates, who is he? Is it any of her crew? You know, that if they should all unite their strength, they could neither move her, nor alter her course a hair's breadth. Who then can it be? But why need I ask? Who can regulate all the motions of the world, except He that made the world? And remember, shipmates, if God is here to regulate her course, he must be here to see how the crew behave.

Once more. Would a wise owner put a crew on board a vessel, and send her to sea, bound on a long voyage, without a compass, chart, quadrant, or pilot, to be driven just where the winds and waves might carry her, till she foundered, or went to pieces on some rocky shore? No, you reply, no wise owner, no man, that cared any thing either for the ship or the ship's company, would act in this manner. And would the good, the all-wise God then, who made the world, and placed us in it, act in such manner? Certainly not. It would be insulting him to think so. You may be certain, therefore, that he has taken care to provide a safe harbor, in which, when the voyage of life is ended, we may ride secure from every danger; that he has furnished us with everything necessary to assist us in shaping our course for that harbor; and that he has provided a skillful pilot, who will carry us into it, if we put ourselves under his care. And, shipmates, we can tell you, for God has told us, that he actually has done all this; As a harbor, he has prepared heaven for us; a place so glorious, that the sun is not fit to be a lamp in it. Could you grasp the world like an orange, and squeeze all the happiness it affords into a single cup, it would be nothing to one drop of the waters of life, which flow there like a river. For a commander and pilot, he has given us his own Son, Jesus Christ, the Captain of salvation; beyond all comparison the most skillful, kind, and careful commander, that ever seaman sailed under. He can carry you, and he alone can carry you safely into the Port of Heaven. No soul ever found its way into that port without him. No soul which put itself under his care, was ever lost. Finally, for a compass, chart, and quadrant, God has given us the Bible; and most completely does it answer the purpose of all three. By this book, as a compass, you may shape your course correctly; for it will always traverse freely, and it has no variation. By this book, as a quadrant, you may at any time, by night or by day, take an observation, and find out exactly where you are. And in this book, as on a chart, not only the Port of Heaven, but your whole course, with every rock, shoal, and breaker, on which you can possibly strike, is most accurately laid down. If then, you make a proper use of this book, mind your helm, keep a good look out, and carefully observe your pilot's directions, you will without fail make a prosperous voyage, and reach the Port of Heaven in safety. It may not, however, be amiss, to give a few hints respecting the first part of your course.

If you examine your chart you will find put down, not far from the latitude in which you now are, a most dangerous rock: called the Rock of Intemperance, or Drunkard's Rock. This rock, on which there is a high beacon, is almost white with the bones of poor sailors who have been cast away upon it. You must be careful to give this rock a good berth, for there is a very strong current setting towards it. If you once get into that current you will find it very difficult getting out again; and will be almost sure to strike it and go to pieces. You will often find a parcel of wreckers round this rock, who will try to persuade you that it is not dangerous, and that there is no current. But take care how you believe them. Their only object is plunder.

Not far from this terrible rock, you will find marked, a whirlpool, almost equally dangerous: called the whirlpool of Bad Company. Indeed this whirlpool often throws vessels upon Drunkard's Rock, as it hurries them round. It lies just outside the Gulf of Perdition; and everything which it swallows up is thrown into that Gulf. It is surrounded by several little eddies, which often draw mariners into it before they know where they are. Keep a good look out then for these eddies, and steer wide of this whirlpool; for it has swallowed up more sailors than ever the sea did. In fact, it is a complete Hell Gate.

Besides this whirlpool and rock, there are several shoals laid down in your chart, which I cannot now stay to describe. Indeed these seas are full of them: which makes sailing here extremely dangerous. If you would be sure to shun them all and to keep clear of the terrible gulf already mentioned, you must immediately go about, make a signal for a pilot, and steer for the Straits of Repentance, which you will see right ahead. These Straits, which are very narrow, form the only passage way out of the dangerous seas you have been navigating, into the great Pacific Ocean, sometimes called the Safe Sea, or Sea of Salvation, on the further shore of which lies your port. It is not very pleasant passing these Straits; and therefore many navigators have tried hard to find another passage. Indeed, some who pretend to be pilots, will tell you there is another; but they are wrong; for the great Master Pilot himself has declared that everyone who does not pass the Straits of Repentance will certainly be lost.

As you pass these Straits, the spacious Bay of Faith will begin to open, on the right hand side of which you will see a high hill, called Mount Calvary. On the top of this hill stands a Lighthouse, in the form of a cross; which, by night, is completely illumined from top to bottom, and by day, sends up a pillar of smoke, like a white cloud. It stands so high, that, unless yon deviate from the course laid down in your chart, you will never lose sight of it in any succeeding part of your voyage. At the foot of this Lighthouse you will find the Pilot I have so often mentioned, waiting for you. You must by all means receive him on board; for without Him, neither your own exertions, nor all the charts and pilots in the world can preserve you from fatal shipwreck.

As you enter the Bay of Faith: you will see, far ahead, like a white cloud in the horizon, the high lands of Hope, which lie hard by your port. These lands are so high, that when the air is clear, you will have them constantly in sight during the remainder of your voyage; and while they are in sight, you may be sure of always finding good anchoring ground, and of safely riding out every storm.

I might proceed to describe the remainder of your course, but it is needless; for you will find it all in your chart, the Bible. With this chart, the society which invited you here this evening, are ready to furnish every destitute seaman; and they do it on purpose that your voyage may be prosperous, and its termination happy. And now, shipmates, let me ask you one question more. Should a ship's crew, bound on a long and dangerous voyage, refuse to provide themselves with either quadrant, chart, or compass: or, being furnished by their owner with these articles, should stow them away in the hold, and never use them, never mind their helm, keep no look out, pay no regard to their pilot's directions, but spend their time in drinking and carousing; have you any doubt that they would be lost, before their voyage was half over? And when you heard that they were lost, would you not say, "It is just as I expected; but they have no one to blame except themselves." Just so, my dear shipmates, if you refuse to receive the Bible, the book which your Maker and owner has given, to assist in shaping your course; or if you lay this book aside in your chests, and never study it; or if you study it, and do not shape your course by it, nor pay any regard to the directions of Jesus Christ, your Commander and Pilot; but make your only object to live an easy, careless, merry life; be assured that you will make shipwreck of your souls, and founder in that gulf which has no bottom; and while you feel that you are lost, lost, lost forever, you will also feel that you have no one to blame for it but yourselves. You cannot blame God, your Creator and Owner; for he has kindly given you his only Son to be your Pilot, and his Book to be your chart. You cannot blame your fellow-creatures; for, by the hands of this Society, they now offer you this book, "without money and without price." You cannot blame the speaker; for he has now told you what will be the consequence of neglecting this book. O, then, be persuaded to receive it, to study it, and to shape your course by it. Become yourselves members of this Bible Society, and persuade your comrades to do the same. Wherever you see the Bethel Flag hoisted, rally round it. As often as you have an opportunity, visit the house of God on the Sabbath, to hear what Jesus Christ has done for poor Seamen. If you see a brother sailor becalmed by the way, or steering another course, lend him a hand, and take him with you. Whenever you are keeping your evening watch on deck, look up, and see the God of whom you have now heard; the God whose name, I fear, some of you "take in vain," enthroned in awful silence, and darkness, and majesty, on the sky, crowned with a diadem of ten thousand stars, holding the winds and thunderbolts in his hand, and setting one foot on the sea, and the other on the land, while both land and sea obey his word, and tremble at his nod. This, shipmates, is the God under whom we wish you to enlist, and to whom we wish you to pray. This is the God who now offers to be the poor sailor's friend; and who, in all your voyages, can carry you out in safety, and bring you home in peace. This too, is the God whom we shall all one day see coming in the clouds of Heaven with power and great glory, to judge the world. Then, at his command, the earth and the sea shall give up all who had been buried in the former or sunk in the latter, and they shall stand together before God to be rewarded according to their works. O then, seamen, landsmen, whoever you are that hear, prepare, prepare for this great day. Yes, prepare, ye accountable creature, prepare to meet your God; for he has said, "Behold I come, I come near to judgment!" And hath he said it, and shall he not do it? Hath He spoken, and shall he not make it good? Yes, when His appointed hour shall arrive, a mighty angel will lift his hand to Heaven, and swear by Him who liveth for ever and ever, that there shall be time no longer. Then our world, impetuously driven by the last tempest, will strike, and be dashed in pieces on the shores of eternity. Hark! what a crash was there! One groan of unutterable anguish, one loud shriek of consternation and despair is heard, and all is still. Not a fragment of the wreck remains to which the struggling wretches might cling for support; but down, down, down they sink, plunged deep beneath the billows of Almighty wrath. But see! something appears at a distance mounting above the waves, and nearing the shore. It is the Ark of salvation! It is the Life Boat of Heaven! It has weathered the last storm; it enters the harbor triumphantly; Heaven resounds with the acclamations of its grateful, happy crew! Among them, may you all, shipmates, be found. May the members of this Society, believing and obeying, as well as distributing the Scriptures, save both themselves and the objects of their care. And may every perishing immortal in this assembly, now, while the Ark is open, while the Life Boat waits, while the rope of mercy is thrown within his grasp, seize it, and make eternal life his own! AMEN.

SCENES FROM HIS SICKBED AND DEATHBED

"The closing months of his life were rendered memorable by an extraordinary triumph of faith and patience, as well as of the power of mind over matter. His bodily suffering and agonies were indescribable, but, like one of the old martyrs in the midst of the flames, he seemed to forget them all in the greatness of his spiritual joy. In a letter written shortly after his death, Mrs. Payson gives a touching account of the tender and thoughtful concern for her happiness which marked his last illness. Knowing, for example, that she would be compelled to part with her house, he was anxious to have a smaller one purchased and occupied at once, so that his presence in it for a little while might make it seem more homelike to her and the children after he was gone. 'To tell you (she adds) what he was the last six memorable weeks would be altogether beyond my skill. All who beheld him called his countenance angelic.' She then repeats some of his farewell words to her. Begging that she would 'not dwell upon his poor, shattered frame, but follow his blessed spirit to the realms of glory,' he burst forth into an exultant song of delight, as if he already saw the King in His beauty!" (*"More Love to Thee,"* p. 8).

After it had become certain that he would never again leave his sick chamber till he was carried out, yet, being unceasingly desirous to benefit his people, he sent a request, which was announced from the pulpit, that they would repair to his chamber. Once, it is believed, they came indiscriminately; at other times in specified classes, including as many as the chamber could contain. When he had addressed them collectively his last most solemn and affectionate counsel, till compelled to desist by the failure of his strength, he took them individually by the hand, and, with a heavenly smile bade them farewell!

To members of his congregation, he spoke nearly as follows:

"It has often been remarked, that people who have been into the other world, cannot come back to tell us what they have seen; but I am so near the eternal world, that I can see almost as clearly as if I were there; and I see enough to satisfy myself, at least, of the truth of the doctrines which I have preached. I do not know that I should feel at all surer, had I been really there.

It is always interesting to see others in a situation in which we know that we must shortly be placed ourselves; and we all know that we must die. And to see a poor creature, when, after an alternation of hopes and fears, he finds that his disease is mortal, and death comes to tear him away from everything he loves, and crowds, and crowds him to the very verge of the precipice of destruction, and then thrusts him down headlong! There he is, cast into an unknown world; no friend, no Savior to receive him.

O, how different is this from the state of a man who is prepared to die. He is not obliged to be crowded reluctantly along; but the other world comes like a great magnet, to draw him away from this; and he knows that he is going to enjoy, and not only knows, but begins to taste it, perfect happiness; forever and ever; forever and ever!

And now God is in this room; I see him; and O, how unspeakably lovely and glorious does he appear, -worthy of ten thousand thousand hearts, if we had them. He is here, and hears me pleading with the creatures that he has made, whom he preserves, and loads with blessings, to love him. And O, how terrible does it appear to me, to sin against this God; to set up our wills in opposition to his, and, when we awake in the morning, instead of thinking, 'What shall I do to please my God today?' to inquire, 'What shall I do to please myself today?'"

After a short pause he continued, "It makes my blood run cold to think how inexpressibly miserable I should now be without religion. To lie here, and see myself tottering on the verge of destruction! O; I should be distracted! And when I see my fellow-creatures liable every moment to be reduced to this situation, I am in an agony for them, that they may escape their danger before it be too late. When people repent, they begin to see God's infinite perfections, how amiable and glorious he is, and the heart relents and mourns that it has treated him so ungratefully.

Suppose we should hear the sound of a man's voice pleading earnestly with someone, but could not distinguish the words; and we should inquire, 'What is that man pleading for so earnestly?' 'O, he is only pleading with a fellow creature to love his God, his Savior, his Preserver and Benefactor. He is only pleading with him not to throw away his immortal soul, not to pull down everlasting wretchedness upon his own head. He is only persuading

him to avoid eternal misery, and accept eternal happiness.'
'Is it possible,' we should exclaim, 'that any persuasion can
be necessary for this?' and yet it is necessary. O my friends,
do, do love this glorious Being; do seek for the salvation of
your immortal souls. Hear the voice of your dying
minister, while he entreats you to care for your souls."

And his dying words to the young men of his congregation were as follows:
"I felt desirous that you might see that the religion I have
preached can support me in death. You know that I have
many ties which bind me to earth: a family to which I am
strongly attached, and a people whom I love almost as well;
but the other world acts like a much stronger magnet, and
draws away my heart from this.

Death comes every night and stands by my bedside
in the form of terrible convulsions, every one of which
threatens to separate the soul from the body. These grow
worse and worse till every bone is almost dislocated with
pain. Yet while my body is thus tortured, the soul is
perfectly, perfectly happy and peaceful. I lie here and feel
these convulsions extending higher and higher, but my soul
is filled with joy unspeakable! I seem to swim in a flood of
glory which God pours down upon me. Is it a delusion that
can fill the soul to overflowing with joy in such circumstances? If so, it is a delusion better than any reality. It is no
delusion. I feel it is not. I enjoy this happiness now. And
now, standing as I do on the ridge that separates the two
worlds; feeling what intense happiness the souls is capable
of sustaining, and judging of your capacities by my own,
and believing that those capacities will be filled to the very
brim with joy or wretchedness forever, my heart yearns
over you, my children, that you may choose life and not

death. I long to present every one of you with a cup of happiness and see you drink it.

A young man just about to leave the world, exclaimed, 'The battle's fought, the battle's fought, but the victory is lost forever!' But I can say, 'The battle's fought, and the victory is won -- the victory is won forever!' I am going to bathe in the ocean of purity, and benevolence, and happiness, to all eternity. And now, my children, let me bless you, not with the blessing of a poor, feeble, dying man, but with the blessing of the infinite God."

He then pronounced the apostolic benediction.

It seems fitting to conclude the brief Legacy of this legend by giving a letter Dr. Payson wrote his sister Eliza a few weeks before his death. It reads,
"Were I to adopt the figurative language of Bunyan I might date this letter from the land of Beulah, of which I have been for some weeks a happy inhabitant. The celestial city is full in my view. Its glories beam upon me, its breezes fan me, its odors are wafted to me, its sounds strike upon my ear, and its spirit is breathed into my heart. Nothing separates me from it but the river of death, which now appears but as an insignificant rill, that may be crossed at a single step, whenever God shall give permission. The Sun of Righteousness has been gradually drawing nearer and nearer, appearing larger and brighter as He approached, and now He fills the whole hemisphere, pouring forth a flood of glory, in which I seem to float like an insect in the beams of the sun, exulting yet almost trembling while I gaze on this excessive brightness, and wondering, with unutterable wonder, why God should deign thus to shine upon a sinful worm. A single heart and a single tongue seem altogether inadequate to my wants; I want a whole heart for every separate emotion, and a whole tongue to express that emotion.

But why do I speak thus of myself and my feelings? why not speak only of our God and Redeemer? It is because I know not what to say. When I would speak of them my words are all swallowed up. I can only tell you what effects their presence produces, and even of these I can tell you but very little. O, my sister, my sister! Could you but know what awaits the Christian; could you know only so much as I know, you could not refrain from rejoicing, and even leaping for joy. Labors, trials, troubles, would be nothing; you would rejoice in afflictions, and glory in tribulations; and, like Paul and Silas, sing God's praises in the darkest night, and in the deepest dungeon. You have known a little of my trials and conflicts, and know that they have been neither few nor small; and I hope this glorious termination of them will serve to strengthen your faith, and elevate your hope.

And now, my dear, dear sister, farewell. Hold on your Christian course but a few days longer, and you will meet in heaven,

Your happy and affectionate brother,

Edward Payson"

And in this precious frame, gazing already upon the Beatific Vision, he passed into glory October 22, 1827 at the tender age of forty-four. May his life and his words be used of the Spirit of God to draw us closer to the precious Son of God and prepare us for that day when we shall appear before the judgment seat of Christ.

APPENDIX ONE

The Testimony of Cyrus Hamlin, Missionary, Educator
read before the Maine Historical Society,
May 10, 1895

I came to Portland in January 1827, on completing my
sixteenth year. Everything was surprisingly new to me and
inspired me to a new sort of life. I had seen one or two
villages of twenty-five to fifty houses. Portland had twelve
to fifteen thousand inhabitants, and to me it was a great
city, a hundred-fold greater than it is now...

But when I came to Portland in 1827, the greatest,
the most unique object of interest was Dr. Payson.
Although his work was nearly done, and he had been
assured by his physicians that he could have little hope of
recovery, yet he preached occasionally with a fervor and
power that left an abiding impression upon the minds of
his hearers. I saw Payson then only during the last nine
and one half months of his heroic conflict with disease. But
no person ever made that impression upon me that he did.
This may have been in part due to his reputation. His own
people all but worshipped him. Other cities offered him
many strong inducements to leave Portland, but he never
heeded them. His saintly character, his failing health,
under the advance of a most painful disease, the general
expectation of his death, his great patience and persistence
in duty, had softened the asperities that had existed. The
tongue of slander was silent. The efforts to injure his
character had rebounded upon the accusers, and men of
various beliefs crowded to hear Payson's last words. As an

arm on one side and a leg on the other were paralyzed, a source of constant and severe pain, there could not be the slightest effort at any of the graces of oratory. Anything of that kind would have been utterly out of place. When it was known that Payson would preach, the church was full at an early hour. He went down the broad aisle supported by one of his deacons, swinging mechanically the paralyzed limb in place, so as to support him in part. He ascended awkwardly, pathetically, if you please, the pulpit stairs, for it drew many tears from those who loved and honored him, and who knew that he was determined to preach so long as power of voice or motion was left to him, in defiance of weakness and suffering.

It was literally going down the broad aisle, for the floor of the church had been elevated in the rear some three or four feet so as to form an inclined plane toward the pulpit. This had been done at his request. It made it easier for him to reach every ear with his voice and every countenance with his eye. He wanted to get into personal relation with every person in his audience.

I saw Dr. Payson only as an invalid under medical condemnation to death. There was nothing in his personal appearance to attract a crowd. He was only a man of ordinary proportions, perhaps slightly above the average in height. He was of dark complexion, had a piercing black eye, with a kindly expression of countenance shaded by constant, uninterrupted suffering. The indifferent observer saw only a crippled man, awkwardly performing a public duty. It might be said to the assembled crowd, "But what went ye out for to see? A reed shaken by the wind?" A broken reed at that.

I recall very distinctly the impression of Payson's voice. It was grave, earnest and clear, so that not a syllable was lost to the listener. You heard every sentence without any effort of attention. A peculiarity of his preaching at that time was his wealth of illustration. He was a man of wide reading, and he had a memory that kept pace with his rapid reading. There was no department of history, science, philosophy or theology that he did not aim to keep up with. He laid all his reading and all his life's experience and observation under tribute for the illustration and enforcement of the truth in hand. His illustrations were natural, unstudied; they came of themselves, but were often so pat as to have the force of logic. There was no such thing as inattention while he was speaking. The truth may have been unpopular, but it was so illustrated and brought within the sphere of the listener's experience that he was eagerly listened to. It was a surprise to me that I understood, or thought I understood, everything that Dr. Payson said. I thought a preacher so distinguished would be far above my comprehension. His thoughts were clear and definite, and so clearly expressed that the young as well as the old could take them in. He intended just that, and they did understand him. I listened for the first time to a sermon that I followed from beginning to end, and felt that in some mysterious way what he said was meant for me, although I knew it was not. His felicity of illustration gave an attractive charm to everything he was trying to enforce, and the earnestness and honesty of his manner and character were above all oratory and rhetoric.

It was, however, in the Bible class that I recall his manner with the greatest distinctness. He held on to that after he had forever left the pulpit. His formal farewell to the pulpit was inexpressibly tender and affecting, and melted the whole audience to tears. One reason given was that he might husband his little remaining strength for the Bible class, which was not designed for the church members, but exclusively for those who had not made a profession of faith. I had attended this exercise from the first Sunday of my being in Portland. There was a strange fascination in it. It was in a long, narrow conference room, and the desk was in the middle of the right-hand side as you entered. I was always in my place about halfway from the door to the desk. The room was always full when Payson entered, and immediately afterward the standing places were all occupied. I sat where I could see every lineament of his countenance. It was unlike any countenance I had ever seen and it made an indelible impress on me. His eye was bright and clear, but there was no muscular (or muscle) life in his face. It was as immobile as though carved from some dark wood. It was a very sad countenance, and the constant heroic determination to repress every outward indication of pain had given that firm, fixed, sculptured look to the lineaments of his face.

After the singing of a hymn and the utterance of a brief, earnest prayer, the work of the hour began; and it was always the work of a master. He exhibited in his instructions a rare knowledge of human nature, or rather of the human heart in all its relations to the great questions of the future life. He knew what was in man. He seemed to have a subtle intuition of all the phases and turns of thought and feeling which were possible in human souls awakened to spiritual thought. His object was to help all thoughtful persons over the difficulties they found in their way in commencing a religious life. He would suppose cases so aptly that every one would find his own case fairly stated and treated.

He knew there were others who came to the meeting with no fixed moral purpose. They were considered in various lights and shades, but always in a way to attract rather than repel. He knew also that some might be present with feelings of positive hostility to the great truths of redemption. He treated such cases with great wisdom and tenderness; never in a way to give any reasonable person any occasion of offense. There was no monotony in the service from week to week. The audience room was always packed. There was something very peculiar in Dr. Payson's prayers or praying. The room became so still that it seemed as though every one had stopped breathing. He seemed to enter into the very presence of God and to bring the divine presence into the room. I used to hear person's speak of Payson's prayers as the most wonderful part of the service. Other men might preach like him but nobody could pray like him.

I have forgotten to say that when he began to speak his countenance gradually changed; it lighted up. His face became mobile and expressive of emotion. His Gethsemane countenance left him and he was on the Mount of Transfiguration. I have no question but the relief from pain was real and absolute for the time. There was a physical change wrought through the mysterious connection of the mind with the body. He had a high conception of the possibilities of every soul for good or ill. Of the three hundred young persons before him he noted every one. He had that capacity of seeing his audience not *en masse* but as individuals, in every one of whom he felt a deep interest and for whose eternal future he must give account to God. He had, in overpowering measure, the feelings of Paul toward the Galatians who travailed in pain for them until Christ should be formed in them. No new face could appear in his large audience, no old face could disappear, without attracting his attention.

As this paper is a mere personal reminiscence, I may be allowed perhaps to introduce my experience on this point of his individual interest in his hearers. When he requested from the pulpit that his church members would not attend the Bible class, as he had been informed that many persons were excluded for want of room, and the exercise was intended expressly for those who were not members of the church, I absented myself as a matter of course, as I thought it not fair that I should go every Sunday and thus exclude some other one. Monday morning a church member came to me in the shop, and taking me aside, said that Dr. Payson had noticed my absence and wished to know if his remark from the pulpit had caused it. I confessed it had. I was sorry to leave, but it did not seem right for me to crowd in and crowd another out. He replied that Dr. Payson's remark was designed to provide room for such as me, and that Dr. Payson wished me to return. It surprised me profoundly that he should have noticed me or thought of me at all, and still more that he should have sent one to look me up. I thought of the good shepherd leaving the ninety and nine to seek but one.

I was in my place the next Sunday before the house was full. It soon became compactly filled except the aisle left open for the doctor. At length he came in, leaning very heavily on Deacon Coe, and was helped into his chair in the desk. With his unparalyzed hand he wiped the perspiration from his face, and then turning to his right he swept his earnest look round to the left, and saw every face that was turned toward him. I am not sure by any means that he looked at me, but he seemed to, and when I looked up he still seemed to be looking at me with a look of welcome, but of concern. It seemed to say, 'You poor little country boy, what is to be your future in the temptations of your new life?' Before he gave out the hymn he wanted to correct a misapprehension. His remark from the pulpit to his church members had been misunderstood by some. Two interesting young strangers had stayed away the last time from that misapprehension. He was glad to see them in their seats again, and hoped if any others had remained away from a like cause they would return. I cannot doubt but one of the two referred to myself. That watchful care, that earnest solicitude, that love that was stronger than death, were more potent appeals than any human eloquence could have been. Time does not efface my memory of them, although nearly seventy years have passed by. Such experiences enter into one's mental and moral being, and form a part of his existence. Present things may make a mere evanescent impression which suddenly fades away, but these never. We lay up our treasures in youth; we enjoy them in old age.

Dr. Payson's ruling passion was strong in death. His triumphant departure is too well known for me to describe it here. When dying he wished to have this message on a slip of paper pinned to his bosom in the casket:

Remember the words that I spoke unto you
while I was present with you.

I fell into the long procession that passed by the casket. I read this inscription. I gave that face one earnest gaze. It looked peaceful and restful, and yet, perhaps, from our own imagination, there was the impress of joyful triumph on his brow. He had fought the good fight, he had finished his course, he had kept the faith, he had gone to receive his crown. This was my farewell to Dr. Payson, my spiritual father, and one of the most distinguished citizens of Portland and of Maine.

APPENDIX TWO

The Ordination Service
conducted on December 16th, 1807

of the
Rev. Edward Payson
as
Colleague Pastor
of the
Second Congregational Church
in
Portland, Maine.

Including the Ordination Discourse
by
Rev. Seth Payson
Pastor of the Church in Rindge, NH

The Charge to the Candidate
by
Rev. Joseph Buckminster
Pastor of the Church in Portsmouth, NH

The Right Hand of Fellowship
by
Rev. Caleb Bradley
Pastor of the Church of Falmouth, ME

ORDINATION DISCOURSE
by
Rev. Seth Payson

*"Lay hands suddenly on no man,
neither be partaker of other men's sins."*
1 Timothy 5:22

The several parts of the divine word have each their respective uses, adapted to the various circumstances and necessities of the church. The epistle, from which the passage now read is selected, was designed to exhibit the nature and importance of the ministerial office, and the manner, in which its sacred duties should be performed. Though particularly directed to Timothy, it is of universal obligation, and all, who acknowledge its divine authority, will feel its precepts equally binding on themselves.

Our text, it is obvious, is one of those passages, on which is founded the sacred rite of the imposition of hands in separating persons to the ministerial office, and the whole work of ordination is here represented by one expressive ceremony, used on that occasion. This passage, therefore, evidently contains a caution against introducing persons suddenly into the gospel ministry, and a reason, with which that caution is enforced. To illustrate these two points is the design of the following observations.

I. In this passage we have a caution against introducing persons into the ministry suddenly, i.e. without first obtaining sufficient evidence, that they are qualified to discharge its important duties. In every concern of human life qualifications are required, suited to the service, in which, men engage, and calculated to promote the object of their exertions; and where we feel our interest concerned, we are careful to employ those only, who are possessed of requisite endowments. To prove that peculiar endowments are requisite to qualify persons for an office so sacred, so arduous, so incomparably important, as that of the ministry, cannot surely be necessary in a Christian assembly. The man, who will not employ a common laborer or mechanic, without being previously convinced of his skill and fidelity, and at the same time will commit his own soul, or the souls of others. to the care of every pretender, is not a subject of argument. Before such persons can be convinced of the madness of their conduct, they must be brought to feel, that the whole world cannot counterbalance the loss of a soul. To those, who are sensible of this, it will be sufficient to suggest, that the greatest calamities, with which the church has ever been afflicted both under the ancient and modern dispensation, have arisen from the introduction of unqualified teachers.

Admitting then that peculiar endowments are necessary to qualify persons for the Christian ministry, to what cause can it be imputed, that many are introduced into this sacred office without even a pretended examination, whether they possess them? By whatever plausible reasons this practice may be supported and whatever may be its ostensible source, it evidently originated from that kingdom, which is hostile to the kingdom of God and his Christ. Why was Timothy so expressly cautioned against conferring ordaining rites suddenly on any man, whatever his profession or appearance, if examination be unnecessary? Or why were the qualifications of the gospel bishop so minutely stated by an inspired writer, as we find them in the epistles of St. Paul, if they are not a rule, by which those, who offer themselves as candidates for this work, are to be tried?

To avoid the evil, against which we are cautioned in our text, it is necessary to ascertain from the law and the testimony, what are the qualifications of a good minister of Jesus Christ. Among these may be mentioned,

First, *a mind exercised in scientific pursuits, and enriched with stores of useful knowledge.* A well cultivated mind evidently possesses peculiar advantages both for acquiring and communicating religious truth, and is, therefore, in some degree necessary to produce that "aptness to teach," which the apostle expressly requires in the gospel minister. Human literature may be considered as the medium of vision, or atmosphere, by which the rays of the sun of righteousness are diffused, and brought to the eye in a manner best suited to the various circumstances and necessities of the spiritual life. Those, who despise the aid of science in the concerns of religion, strangely forget, that it is the vehicle, which God has chosen for publishing the blessed truths of his gospel, and that, without its assistance, the scriptures must to us have remained a sealed book. But the apostles, we shall be told, were illiterate men. It is granted, that with some exceptions they were so, but it must be remembered, that this defect was supplied not only by the personal instructions of our Savior, but also by the gift of tongues, and other miraculous powers. So time was, when God fed his people with bread from heaven, but is it therefore a just inference, that they do not now need a supply of food from the earth? Still, however, it must be understood, that science is necessary only as a mean, by which the acquisition and communication of religious truth is facilitated, and not as a substitute for divine teaching. For the absence of this, no natural or acquired abilities will in any degree compensate. We, therefore, proceed to observe,

Second, that he, who is ordained to teach others the way of life and salvation, *must himself be taught of God, and made experimentally acquainted with that gospel, of which he is constituted a minister.* We are plainly taught in the divine word, that the hearts of mankind in their natural state are enmity against the laws, the government, and character of Jehovah; that they neither approve nor understand the things of his spirit; and, that their feelings are in direct opposition to the gospel of his Son. That such men are qualified to promote a reconciliation between God and sinners is a sentiment as absurd in itself, as it has been found pernicious in its consequences. It must be obvious to every unprejudiced mind, that the ambassadors of Christ ought to be his real friends, and to have experienced the enlightening and sanctifying influences of his Spirit. This, however, is a sentiment of too much importance to be left unsupported by evidence. Sufficient proof of its truth may easily be drawn from a cursory view of the duties of the Christian minister, as it will thence appear, that these duties necessarily imply the existence of a gracious principle in the heart.

Thus for instance it is expressly required of the ministers of Christ, that they should be an example to believers in charity, faith, and purity. But how is he to comply with this requisition, who is himself destitute of these graces? A spirit of Christian prudence, meekness, gentleness, and patience, is also represented as highly important in the ministerial character. "Behold," says our Lord to his disciples, "I send you forth as lambs among wolves; be ye therefore wise as serpents, and harmless as doves." "The servant of the Lord," we are also told, "must not strive, but be gentle unto all men, in meekness instructing those that oppose themselves." These virtues are indispensably necessary, and they can be acquired only in the school of Christ.

Faithfulness is another essential requisite in the character of the true ministers of Jesus Christ; and hence they are by St. Paul compared to stewards, in whose office this virtue is peculiarly necessary. For the same reason he charges Timothy with great solemnity, "to commit the gospel to faithful men." By faithful men he evidently intended men prepared to preach the gospel in the face of opposition, persecution, and death; men true to the cause they had professedly espoused, and wholly devoted to the advancement of the Redeemer's kingdom. In perfect conformity with this idea of faithfulness, the true minister of Christ is represented as superior to selfish views; as one, who seeks not the wealth or applause, but the souls of his people; who preaches not himself, but Christ Jesus the Lord; and who disregards alike the frowns and flatteries of the world. "Do I yet please men," the apostle inquires, adding, "for, if I yet pleased men, I should not be the servant of Christ." Elsewhere indeed he tells us, that he endeavored "to please all men for their good to edification;" but this apparent contradiction only renders still more clear and striking the view of the ministerial character, which is now before us. Indifferent to the applause of mankind, he neither desired nor endeavored to please them for his own sake, yet still, when duty required, he cheerfully sacrificed his Christian liberty to the humors and prejudices of those around him, not to subserve any selfish views, but to promote the success of the gospel, and the salvation of souls.

A readiness to make every possible exertion; to spend and be spent in the service of Christ, is also required of those, who are admitted into the gospel vineyard. They are often spoken of as laborers and workmen; as laborers in time of harvest, when peculiar exertions are necessary. "Meditate upon these things, give thyself wholly to them; be instant in season and out of season; endure hardness as a good soldier of Jesus Christ," is the stimulating language of St. Paul to his son Timothy; injunctions, which were fully exemplified in the painful and unceasing labors of this fervent apostle.

The ambassadors of Christ are also described as possessing a variety of holy affections, suited to the circumstances of those around them. This observation may easily be illustrated from the great pattern of ministerial excellence just mentioned. The main spring of action in his heart was the love of Christ, which, he tells us, constrained him; bore him away as an irresistible torrent, the force of which nothing could withstand or divert. Nor was he less distinguished for love to mankind, and a zeal for their salvation. "I could wish myself accursed from Christ," he cries, when reflecting on the unbelief of his country- men, "for my brethren, my kinsmen according to the flesh." We are not indeed to suppose, that he preferred his countrymen to his Savior; for this would be inconsistent with the character of a Christian. But, without attempting to ascertain the precise meaning of this expression, it must convey to every mind an idea of the most fervent and affectionate concern for their souls. What ardent desires for promoting the salvation of men appear also in the follow- ing expressions, for the truth of which he appeals to witnesses then present. "I have kept back nothing that was profitable to you, but have shewed you, and taught you publicly and from house to house; by the space of three years I ceased not to warn every one of you night and day with tears."

With respect to his spiritual children how tender were his emotions! how dear were they to his heart! how gratefully did he adore the grace of God in them! how fervently did he long and labor for their advancement in the divine life and how deeply was he grieved when he saw disorders arising in the church! Was any part of the Christian body wounded? this feeling member sympathized in the calamity. "Who," says he, "is weak, and I am not weak ? Who is offended and I burn not?" Did the poverty of those among whom he labored, deprive him of that support, to which he ever asserted his just claim? he then could say, "these hands have ministered to my necessities." Or did those, to whom he ministered in spiritual things, communicate to his relief? In the same flow of holy affection he declares, that his own personal comfort was nothing in his view, compared with the satisfaction of seeing them exhibiting a right temper, and the fruits of— holiness.

This statement of ministerial duty, it will be recollected, is here introduced to prove, that none but men of real piety, are qualified to discharge the duties of an ambassador of Christ, and that consequently on those only, who appear to be men of this character, we can lawfully confer ordaining rites. And is not the proof complete? Are these virtues to be found in unsanctified nature? With equal reason may we expect to gather grapes from thorns, or to see figs produced by a thistle.

Third, another essential qualification in those, who are ordained to preach the gospel, is *soundness in the faith*. The gospel is a system of truth, which, when clearly understood, and cordially embraced, changes the views, feelings, and temper of the soul into a conformity with itself. With the greatest propriety, therefore, is the divine word compared to seed sown in the earth, which propagates its own nature and likeness. To this word of truth the renovation of the soul is expressly ascribed, and believers are represented as "born not of corruptible seed, but of incorruptible, even of the word of God, which liveth and abideth forever." This transforming energy the gospel of Christ alone possesses, and an attempt to enlighten and warm the earth with a painted sun would not be more fruitless and absurd, than that of forming men to holiness by another gospel. Human philosophy and the wisdom of the world had long in vain endeavored to remedy the disorders of our nature, when the Son of God came to bear witness to the truth, and the words, which he spoke, are found by experience to be spirit, and to be life. To cloud this glory of his gospel, and pave the way for the progress of error, the powers of infidelity are now laboring to persuade the world, that it is of little consequence, what we believe and that truth or error, embraced with sincerity, is equally conducive to salvation. Our only protection from this subtle device, we shall find, in carefully observing the inspired direction "to speak the things, which become sound doctrine, and to commit the same to faithful men, who shall be able to teach others also." Our attention is now called,

II. To the reason, with which the apostle enforces upon Timothy the foregoing caution, which is, that, by introducing persons suddenly into the ministerial office, we become partakers of their sins. When unqualified men assume the sacred function, they unavoidably incur great and aggravated guilt. They run without being sent, they seize what God denies them, and break down the barriers which he has raised for the protection of his church. Shall the friends of Christ then countenance the bold invasion, and thus prostitute the powers, with which they are invested for the security of Zion? This they can never do without deeply participating in the guilt of the sacrilegious invader. Nor is it in the guilt of a single transgression only, that such unfaithful watchmen participate, for the mode of expression in the text plainly intimates, that they are partakers in a plurality of sins. It considers them as accountable not only for their own unfaithfulness, but for the endless succession of evils, of which it is the source. It is easy to predict the consequence, when blind men follow blind leaders, or when the care of the flock is committed to ravenous wolves in sheep's clothing. Yet by these expressive images does the word of God represent the pernicious effects of committing the ministry of reconciliation to unqualified men, and especially to those, who are unreconciled to God. For these effects we are answerable, when in consequence of our unfaithfulness, such men are admitted into the ministerial office. We thus become accessory to all the errors, which they bring into the Church; to all the false ideas of religion, which they disseminate; to all the reproach and dishonor they reflect on the cause of Christ; to all the prejudices against his ministers; which their conduct excites; and to the destruction of those souls, who perish: through their ignorance, sloth; or infidelity. Let us not then, by neglecting the caution in our text, expose ourselves to such complicated guilt. We may not indeed be able to detect the concealments of hypocrisy, but we are not therefore excusable in neglecting that examination, of which we are capable.

The undesigned length of the preceding observations precludes several proposed inferences, and renders it necessary to confine the observations, which remain, to those, to whom custom and propriety call our more particular attention.

To us, my Fathers and Brethren who are invested with the powers of ordination, the present subject is peculiarly interesting. We are set for the defense of the gospel; but do we defend it when we employ the rites of ordination in introducing persons into the ministry, without inquiring whether they are for Christ, or against him; whether they sow good seed, or tares in the field; whether they preach Christ crucified, or another gospel? Do we sufficiently consider the evils, resulting from the hasty imposition of hands and the pernicious consequences of introducing into the church, I will not say, immoral men, but men who never felt the worth of a soul, and who appear to be unacquainted with those doctrines, which are necessary to convince mankind of their guilty helpless condition, of their need of a Savior, and of those influences of the divine spirit, by which alone the heart is formed to that holiness, without which no one will see the Lord? Should our minds be impressed with a sense of the importance of a closer attention to the part of ministerial duty, the present opportunity will not be found unprofitable.

A more particular application of this subject is due to the pastor elect. In fulfilling his purposes of mercy to our apostate race, it has pleased a sovereign God to constitute an order of men to preach the unsearchable riches of Christ, and thus to cooperate with himself in accomplishing that object, upon which his adorable Son came into our world. That it is permitted me to assist in introducing you, my dear son, into this highly favored number, as a fellow-worker with God in this glorious design, is an act of his grace, for which I hope our hearts are unitedly adoring his sovereign love. How astonishing is the goodness of God to his unworthy creatures! How great the honor of being admitted to share in the glory of that work which is all his own! This, however, is not the hour of triumph. Your feelings, I hope, accord with that maxim of wisdom; "Let not him who girdeth on the harness boast himself as he that putteth it off." Under the wise and holy government of God, no station or office confers honor, but in connection with a faithful discharge of its duties. If we would obtain that honor which cometh from God only, it must be by "patient continuance in well doing." The glories which now crown the human nature of the Lord Jesus Christ, were won in the field of battle. They are the just reward of invincible virtue and unexampled benevolence. To be admitted into the number of his ministers, is honorable for this reason only, that we are thus brought into the field, where the highest honor is to be won; where all the virtuous feelings of the heart have full play; and where an opportunity is afforded of bringing into action all the energies of the soul, in a service most intimately connected with the glory of God, and the salvation of mankind. In this distinguished station, we are eminently a spectacle to the world, to angels, and to men.

Your path of duty is made plain by the light both of precept and example. Every motive which can influence the human mind prompts you to fidelity, and for your encouragement to go boldly forward in the line of duty, almighty love opens its inexhaustible stores of wisdom, grace, and strength, inviting you to draw near and receive according to your necessities. The object of the observations, which have now been made, is to impress you with a sense of the importance of investigating, so far as human imperfection will admit, the characters and qualifications of candidates for the ministerial office. To me this subject appears of vast, and, from the character of the age in which we live, of increasing importance. It is far from being my wish to see you contending for particular forms of expressing divine truth, or zealously engaged in supporting points, respecting which, through remaining imperfection, wise and good men are divided. This is far beneath the dignified object, which ought to engage the attention of the Christian minister. But, if my most earnest entreaties, if a father's solemn charge, have any influence, never will you be induced to employ the powers of ordination, with which you are now to be invested, in raising the enemies of God and his truth to the pernicious eminence of teachers in the Christian church. In pursuing this leading object, it has been my aim to present to your mind the distinguishing characteristics of the pastor after God's own heart. I hope no earthly attainment appears in your view so desirable as that meekness and faithfulness, that superiority to selfish views, and those fervent, holy, disinterested affections, of which a sketch has now been exhibited. May they ever be the sole objects of your ambition, and be pursued with all that ardor, activity, diligence, and perseverance, with which the children of this world pursue its pleasures, its honors, and wealth.

In laboring to form your mind to ministerial fidelity, may I not hope for some assistance from that active principle of filial affection, which has ever rendered you studious of a father's comfort? I can think with calmness, nay, with a degree of pleasure, of your suffering for righteousness' sake, and, should the world pour upon you its obloquy, its scorn and reproach, for your fidelity to your Master's cause, a father's heart would still embrace you with, if possible, increased fondness. But to see you losing sight of the great objects which ought to engage your attention, courting the applause of the world, infected with the infidel sentiments of the day, and neglecting the immortal interests of those now about to be committed to your care; this, O my son, I could not support. It would bring down my gray hairs with sorrow to the grave. But is it possible, that in such a cause, with such motives to fidelity, and with prospects, may I not add, so peculiarly pleasing as those which now surround you, you should, notwithstanding, prove unfaithful? It is possible; for there is nothing too base, too ungrateful, or destructive of our own most important interests, for human nature to commit; and, unless the grace of the Lord Jesus preserve you, the glory of God will be forgotten, your Savior will by you be crucified afresh, and his cause exposed to shame; your sacred character will become your reproach, and, instead of the blessings of many ready to perish, you will accumulate the curses of perishing souls upon your head. May your preservation from this awful fate be the theme of our future eternal praises.

Contemplating the sublimity of the apostolic pattern, do you ask, 'How shall I attain to such activity, such zeal, such purity, such disinterestedness, and ardor of affection?' Remember Paul was nothing. He himself makes the confession. "It is not I," says he, "that live, but Christ, that liveth in me; and the life which I now live in the flesh, I live by faith on the Son of God." Thus you may live; thus you may come off more than a conqueror, and, though in yourself but a worm, may thresh the mountains of opposition, and beat them small as the dust. Should the blessed Redeemer grant, and grant he will, if you seek them, the influences of his Spirit, your happy soul will mount up as on eagles' wings, and rise to all those heights of holy affection, to which the great apostle soared. But I must set bounds to the effusion of feelings, which have, perhaps, already exhausted the patience of this assembly. Receive my dear son, in one word the sum of all a father's fond wishes; "Be thou faithful unto death."

To you, Reverend Kellogg, the existing pastor of this church, I now commend one so dear both in flesh and in the Lord. I should be insensible to the proofs of friendship, you have already shown him, did I not feel confident, that he will still enjoy the benefits of your paternal care. Painfully deprived, as from situation I must be, of the delightful interchange of parental and filial duties, it is my solacing hope, that, while he serves with you as a son in the gospel, the assistance of your wisdom and experience will never be withheld, and that increasing measures of light and heat, animation and success, will be the effect of your united labors in this part of the vineyard of our Lord.

To you, Reverend Sir, and the Christian church and society, who statedly worship in this place, we would express our high approbation of your united exertions in seeking additional assistance, proportionate to the increasing field of labor. We most cordially rejoice with you in the unanimity, which has attended your proceedings, and especially in those influences of the divine Spirit, with which you have been favored, and which have rendered the word read and preached effectual to call up the attention of the thoughtless, and produce the glories of the new creation in so many hopeful instances. Amidst these adorable displays of majesty and grace, may you, my Christian friends, be prepared by deep humility and fervent supplications to meet your God, and, with admiring gratitude, welcome the healing manifestations of his almighty power.

It is with emotions, which cannot be expressed, that I contemplate this society as the field, where one, in whose concerns I am so deeply interested, is to exert his labors. To your kindness and friendship I affectionately commend him, and permit me to add, that, while he faithfully discharges the duties of his station, he will have a claim to your candor, your confidence, your prayers, and obediential acquiescence in the declarations, which he shall make to you, of the divine will.

Are Christians at the present day duly sensible of the obligations they are under to cooperate with their pastors; and, by every possible means, to countenance, strengthen, and encourage them in their work? And do they consider how much the success of their labors depends on this? Even the apostles themselves needed the assistance of private Christians, whom we often find them calling upon to unite their prayers and efforts for promoting the great objects of the gospel ministry.

We wish you, brethren, particularly to remember, that, not on your pastors alone, but on you in connection with them, rests the important duty of maintaining the purity of the gospel of Christ, a duty of peculiar importance at a time like the present, when the powers of infidelity are striving by various modes of attack to subvert or corrupt the faith of the gospel; and when many are to be found even in our churches, who, instead of actively defending the great truths of revelation, openly countenance suspicious characters, and even such, as are known advocates of the most dangerous errors. Can conduct like this be consistent with the Christian duty of contending earnestly for the faith once delivered to the saints? Or have those, who are guilty of it, duly considered the apostolic injunction? "If there come any unto you, and bring not this doctrine, receive him not into your house, neither bid him God speed; for he who biddeth him God speed, is a partaker of his evil deeds."

A church, established on gospel principles, united in gospel truth, maintaining gospel discipline, and distinguished by a holy peculiarity of temper and conduct from the surrounding world, is an object, which cannot but deeply interest the feelings of all, who love the Lord Jesus Christ in sincerity. In such a society we see the visible body of the Redeemer, the fruits of his glorious undertaking, and the future members of that illustrious assembly, which St. John in vision, saw standing on mount Zion, having their father's name written in their foreheads. Such an interesting spectacle may you, my dear brethren, ever exhibit. May you enjoy much of that anointing, which is from above. May you ever walk worthy of your high and holy vocation, maintain the order and discipline of Christ's house, and exemplify in your lives and conversation the lovely graces of pure and undefiled religion. Remembering, that peace and harmony constitute your beauty and strength, may you and your united pastors faithfully discharge the militant duties of this state of trial, and be hereafter presented faultless to join the church triumphant in heavenly glory.

The subject will be closed with a short address to this numerous assembly. The exhortation in the text has indeed a primary reference to those only, who are called to the work of the ministry; but at the same time it points out the path of duty to all, who are concerned in the choice of a minister. In his word God has graciously given that instruction, which is necessarily to direct you in the use of the privilege you enjoy, of choosing your own teachers. Will you then madly counteract his merciful design by countenancing those men from whom he is endeavoring to preserve you? If you fly from those, who tell you the truth; who with friendly earnestness admonish you of your guilty, miserable state; who endeavor to demolish your false hopes, and direct your steps to the strait gate and narrow way, which leads to life; and seek for your guides those, who will flatter your corruptions, prophecy smooth things, and cry, "Peace, peace", when there is no peace; what can you expect, but, with your blind leaders, to plunge into the pit of destruction? A person preferring a luscious poison to the unpalatable, but salutary prescriptions of a kind and skillful physician, affords but a faint emblem of the folly of those, who choose that instruction, which causeth to err. What light is to darkness, what the pure grain is to chaff, such is truth, when compared with falsehood. Buy then the truth, nor suffer any thing to deprive you of the precious gem.

Do you ask with Pilate, "what is truth?" Then hear. *It is truth,* that there is a God, sovereign, holy, just, and true, infinite in goodness and mercy, but who will by no means clear the guilty. *It is truth,* that this God, the creator of all things, is the former of our bodies, and the father of our spirits; that he has nourished and brought us up as children; that we have rebelled against him, have violated his law, and become exposed to its curse. *It is truth,* that God so loved the world as to give up his only begotten

Son, in whom dwells all the fulness of the godhead bodily, to redeem us from the curse of the law, by being made a curse for us. *It is truth,* that he, who believeth on the Son of God, hath everlasting life, and that he, who believeth not the Son, shall not see life, but the wrath of God abideth on him. *It is truth,* that, unless we repent, we must unavoidably perish; that, except a man be born again, he cannot see the kingdom of God; that, if any man be in Christ, he is a new creature; and, that without holiness no man shall see the Lord. *It is truth,* that we must all appear before the judgment seat of Christ, where a doom, far more intolerable than that of guilty Sodom, will be the portion of those, who hear, but neglect the offers of salvation. These things, in the name of the great God, I testify to you, are truth; and may the almighty energies of his Spirit so impress these truths upon your hearts, that you may become wise unto eternal life.   - AMEN

THE CHARGE

by

Rev. Joseph Buckminster

God all-sufficient needeth not us, nor any of our services, neither can we be profitable to him, as he who is wise may be to himself; yet hath it pleased him to administer his government, and dispense his grace through the medium of instrumental agents. That scheme of religion, which combines and displays all the perfections of Deity, and which is emphatically styled *the glorious gospel of the blessed God,* which began to be preached by the Lord from heaven, and is confirmed unto us by them that heard it, is in its successive dispensation, entrusted to the ministry of favored individuals of that race for whom its grace was provided. "We have this treasure in earthen vessels, that the excellency of the power may be of God and not of us." To guard his own honor, to aid our infirmities, and detect the delusions of error and enthusiasm, he has published, and put into our hands, a complete system of truth and duty, dictated by his Spirit, and sealed with his own seal, willful departure from which is high treason against heaven.

The great head of the church, the king in Zion, does not send us to publish any new truths; nor to enjoin any new duties. To explain and enforce what are already given is the extent of our commission, accompanied with this admonition, "Call no man master upon earth, for one is your master, even Christ, and all ye are brethren." In giving the charge therefore, on ordination occasions, we would not be understood to claim any authority to dictate,

155

nor right to prescribe to our younger brother, the doctrine he must preach, or the duties he must inculcate and perform; our object is to bring to his recollection, and to impress upon his conscience and our own, a summary of the charge which we believe our divine Lord, by himself and his inspired apostles, has given to all, who desire the *good work* of a bishop, and are entering upon that important office.

This friendly and paternal part of the solemnities of the day, the ecclesiastical council have assigned to me.

Permit me then, my young friend, to stir up your pure mind by way of remembrance, and as the organ of the council, admonish you, on this day of your ministerial consecration to *take heed to yourself.* See that your heart be right with God, clothed with humility, and impressed with adoring awe of his matchless majesty, that you be in a state of favor and reconciliation with him; a loyal subject, a real disciple, a faithful servant of the Lord Jesus Christ. Let not his livery cover a heart of treason, nor exhibit false signals to his church and people. Be correct in the views, principles, and motives with which you enter on your ministry. Mistake not the spirit of Jehu, for the spirit of Jesus, nor those gifts and graces, which ministers may receive for the benefit of the church, for that special grace which proves our adoption into the family or God. Take heed to yourself in reference to your whole conduct, ministerial, social, and secular. Know how to behave yourself in the house of God, which is the church of the living God. Let your air and deportment be such as become the presence of the living God, and the sacred solemnities of his house, such as preceding communion with God would naturally produce, and the power of sympathy will tend to diffuse. Let your common conversation be always with grace seasoned with salt, such as may minister grace to the hearers. Set before you the example of our divine Master, who secluded not himself from the social walks of life, but rendered it the fault of every circle he met, if they were not wiser and better for the interview. "Be thou an example to the believer in word, in conversation, in charity, in spirit, in faith, in purity."

Religiously discipline your worldly desires and hopes. Seek not great things to yourself in a world that is evil, corrupt, and devoted to destruction, the vanity of which you are continually to proclaim. While you charge those that are rich in this world, that they trust not in uncertain riches, see that your own heart be free from that love of money which is the root of evil, and which is sometimes found where very little of it is possessed. Entangle not yourself, unnecessarily, in any secular pursuits, lest they interrupt your reading, meditation, and prayer, and prevent your profiting in the things of religion. Degrade not the dignity of your station and the sacredness of your office, by giving the slightest ground of suspicion, that you would render them subservient to more selfish or secular purposes. "O thou man of God, flee these things; and follow after righteousness, godliness, faith, love, patience, meekness." "*Give no offense in any thing*, that the ministry be not blamed."

A discreet attention to this part of your charge will facilitate your observance of the second material branch, *taking heed to your doctrine*. You are put in trust with the gospel, with the ministry of reconciliation, the constituted vehicle of grace, and it "hath pleased God, by the foolishness of preaching, to save them that believe." Preach then, my brother, the *word of God*. In doctrine show uncorruptness, gravity, sincerity, and sound speech. Declare the whole counsel of God, so far as you can satisfactorily discern it, in the sacred scriptures. In meekness instruct those that oppose themselves; but keep back nothing that may be profitable to men. Amuse not immortal souls with uninteresting speculations. Surprise them not with flights of imagination unwarranted by Scripture, nor with any parade of science, *falsely* so called. Court not a smile, nor strive to awaken wonder, when you would impress the conscience of a sinner, or win a soul to Christ. Be not weary in well doing. Preach the word, be instant in season and out of season, feed Christ's sheep, and feed his lambs. Reprove, rebuke, and exhort with all long-suffering and doctrine, and with gravity and authority which shall secure from contempt.

To know the state of your flock is another part of your charge, which your pastoral visits wisely conducted will greatly facilitate, and will probably be the mean of strengthening affection, and of reciprocating instruction and consolation. As the minister of him who came to bind up the broken hearted, know how to comfort the feeble in mind and to support the weak. By the bed of sickness, and in the abodes of sorrow, show that you have the heart of sympathy and the tongue of experience; study to find acceptable words, being words of truth; "words fitly spoken are like apples of gold in pictures of silver."

You are constituted a ruler in the house of God, and, in connection with our elder brother with whom by an unusual concurrence of providences, you are called to minister in the gospel as a son with a father, you are charged to keep the ordinances as they are delivered unto you; and to administer them to proper subjects. In exercising that discipline which Christ hath instituted for edification, and not for destruction, let nothing be done by partiality or under the influence of prejudiced and passionate views. Have no man's person in admiration because of advantage, neither grind the faces of the poor.

Let private admonition and affectionate exhortation as much as possible supersede public censure and let charity cover a multitude of sins. But let offenders incorrigible by these discreet endeavors, be rebuked before all that others also may fear. It is a duty of the office with which you are now invested to transmit to faithful men what you have received. The churches to whom we minister will soon need a return of the ministerial service, which the united wish of this pastor and people has called us in a sense to antedate for them. We are not suffered to continue by reason of death, but the promise of the Savior secures a succession of ministers. In ordination solemnities, lay hands suddenly on no man. The things which you have received commit to none but those whom you conceive to be faithful men able to teach others, and likely to answer the important purposes of their sacred separation.

This, my brother, is a summary of the charge which Christ, by his apostles, has given to his ministers, and we exhort and charge you to receive it, with a solemnity becoming the presence of Him who walketh in the midst of his golden candlesticks, and to keep it without spot unrebukable till the appearing of our Lord Jesus Christ.

If in the view of the solemnity and extent of this charge your mind falter and your spirits fail, remember Christ does not send you into this warfare at your own charges, nor lay this weight of responsibility upon you, without promising you guidance and support. "Lo, I am with you always even unto the end of the world." Animated by this promise, may you with meekness gird on the ministerial armor; use it skillfully and successfully, and when you are called to put it off, be able, through grace, to adopt the triumph of the apostle, "I have fought a good fight, I have finished my course, I have kept the faith."

The

RIGHT HAND OF FELLOWSHIP

by

Rev. Caleb Bradley

"Go ye, therefore, and teach all nations, baptizing them in the name of the Father, and of the Son, and of the Holy Ghost. Teaching them to observe all things whatsoever I have commanded you: and lo, I am with you always, even unto the end of the world."

That the gospel of Christ might be dispensed through every age the ministry was instituted and the aids, influences and blessings of the Spirit of Christ, were promised by himself, to be with those, who should preach his gospel until time should be no more.

This institution of our common Lord the Great Head of the church, is wonderfully calculated, under the influences of his Spirit, to reform the vicious, rectify the mistakes, cure the prejudices, and make men wise unto salvation.

The faithful ministers of the blessed Jesus, are under the influence of the same unerring spirit, and joint laborers in the same common cause. It highly becomes them, therefore, as ambassadors of the Lord Jesus Christ, to unite in disseminating the seeds of virtue, and collectively and individually, recommend themselves to every man's conscience in the sight of God, by manifesting, at all times that they are the disciples of the Lord Jesus.

160

It was a custom among the apostles, to present those whom they inducted to the ministerial office with the right hand as a token of their fraternal affection, and as an acknowledgment of their equality, and as being invested with all the privileges and powers attached to their order.

James, Cephas and John, being satisfied that Paul and Barnabas were called by God to dispense the word of his grace, gave to them their right hand of fellowship, and welcomed them into the vineyard of God.

This ceremony has been preserved in the church in every age; and those who have been orderly introduced and received into the ministry, have been acknowledged and received by the churches, by giving them their right hand of fellowship.

Dear Sir, you having given satisfactory evidence of your call to preach the gospel, and having received a charge so to do, it remains only to be acknowledged by this Ecclesiastical Council, that you are initiated into office according to the order of the gospel.

I, therefore in their name, and by their request give you my Right Hand, as a token of our fraternal and ministerial affection for you, and as bidding you welcome into this part of the vineyard of our common Lord.

By this ceremony, we acknowledge you as an ambassador of Christ, regularly introduced into his special service, invested with the same powers and entitled to the same right, with those of us, who previous to this, have been honored with the ministerial office.

We promise you our friendship, and shall do all in our power to encourage your heart and strengthen your hands; so long as your conduct is worthy the office you now hold; expecting you will manifest the like friendship towards us, so long as we conduct ourselves as the disciples of Jesus.

Difficulties and trials you will be likely to meet with in the course of your ministry; but let none of these things move you, neither count your life dear unto yourself, so that you may finish your course with joy, and the ministry you have now received of the Lord Jesus, to testify of the gospel of the grace of God.

If you be actuated from right motives, and walk by faith, and not by sight; if you be under the influence of religion and be established upon the doctrines of the Lord Jesus Christ; if you be as wise as a serpent, harmless as a dove, and as bold as a lion; in a word, if you preach Jesus Christ and him crucified, possessing Christian fortitude and unabating perseverance; you may rest assured, that your Master, whom you have this day promised to serve will be with you, and afford you much of the consolations of his Spirit; for he saith, "Lo, I am with you always."

Now may the God of all grace mercy and peace be with you; may he make you a lasting blessing to the people of your charge; and when he shall call you to quit the present scene of things, may he admit you into the abodes of eternal peace.

We congratulate the church and congregation in this place on the present pleasing prospect.

We rejoice to see so much peace, love, and harmony among you. Long, very long, may you know by happy experience, how good and how pleasant it is for brethren to dwell together in unity.

We wish you much comfort and happiness, in him whom you have this day received, and who has in so solemn a manner been ordained over you as Colleague Pastor, in the work of the ministry.

May he be remembered by you, when you shall address the throne of grace. Pray for him. Supplicate the Father of all mercies on his behalf, that the arms of his hands, may be made strong by the hands of the mighty God of Jacob.

Use your endeavors to make him comfortable and happy. Attend upon his ministry, and forsake not the assembling of yourselves together as the manner of too many is at the present day. Be charitable and hear with candor, and let it appear that he labors not in vain among you, or spends his strength for naught. This will encourage him to persevere in the ways of well-doing. This will give him life and animation, that he may perform more to your acceptance and to the approbation of his Judge, and may God Almighty bless you all from his holy hill of Zion.

Finis

RECOMMENDED READING ON PAYSON

The Complete Works of Edward Payson
Sprinkle Publications, PO Box 355, Bridgewater, VA 22812
sprinkle@rica.net

Revival & Revivalism:
The Making and Marring of American Evangelicalism, 1750-1858
by Iain Murray
The Banner of Truth Trust
3 Murrayfield Road, Edinburgh EH12 6EL
PO Box 621, Carlisle, PA 17013, USA

More Love to Thee: The Life and Letters of Elizabeth Prentiss
by George Lewis Prentiss
Calvary Press Publishing, PO Box 805, Amityville, NY 11701
calvrypres@aol.com

SOLID GROUND CHRISTIAN BOOKS

Solid Ground Christian Books is a publishing venture that is determined to find and publish the very best books ever written. We are convinced that many of the best works of the past remain unknown and unavailable to the people of God. It is our goal to search out those works that God has been pleased to use in the past and bring them out once again before the people of God.

SGCB is committed to the doctrinal foundation of the great Reformation of the 16th century: *Grace Alone, Faith Alone, Christ Alone, Scripture Alone and God's Glory Alone.*

To assure that this publishing business remains on track we have established a Board of Pastoral Reference to oversee the direction of this work. These men have served the Lord faithfully for many years, and we delight to give their names.

Seeking to Spread the Fame of the Name of the Lord
Visit us at http://solid-ground-books.com
E-mail us at solid-ground-books@juno.com
Call us at 205-978-9469